Japanese
BIBLE

Japanese
BIBLE

Fiona Hammond

Contents

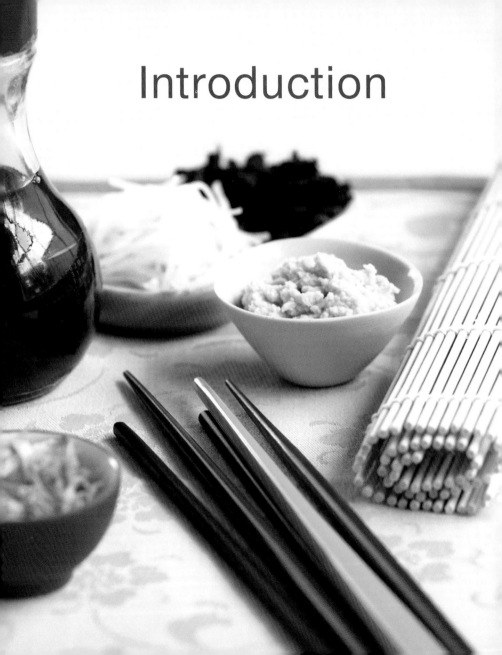

Introduction

Nature is the foundation of Japanese cooking – the focus is to prepare food that tastes and looks as natural as possible. This principle, along with Japan's geography, religion, and interaction with other civilisations over many centuries, has given rise to a unique cuisine.

Food is an integral part of Japanese life; whether at home, at the sushi and noodle bars, or at traditional festivals. There is a simplicity in the style of cooking that makes it accessible to the home cook. But despite its simplicity, Japanese cuisine aspires to perfection – quality ingredients, considered preparation and attractive presentation combine to satisfy all the senses.

Japanese cooks prefer to retain the individual qualities of the ingredients they use, and tend to prepare several dishes for each meal. Seasonings (seaweed, bonito, soy sauce, sake) are subtly employed to enhance the natural flavour of the chosen ingredient. Japanese food is a constant reminder and reflection of the country's beautiful landscape, surrounding seas and cultural traditions.

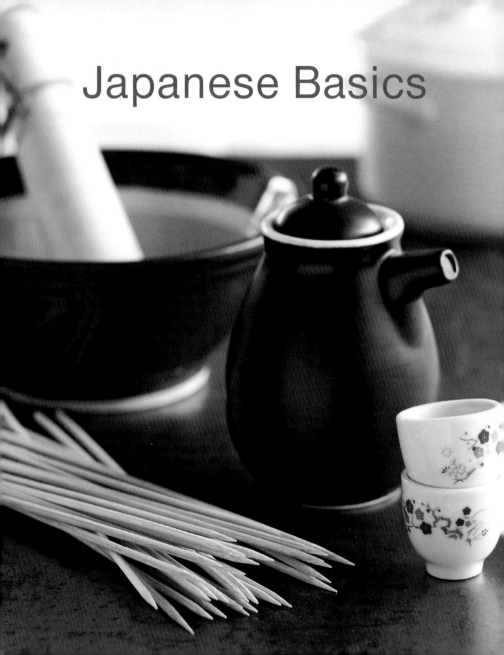

Japanese Basics

Limited by its mountainous terrain, Japan has never produced a large number of crops. Rice and vegetables, and seafood from the surrounding waters, have always been the ingredients most readily available. These limitations have informed the characteristic Japanese approach to food – eating fresh, simply and sparingly.

From the 6th century, Japan came under the influence of China's older, sophisticated culture. Buddhism was introduced, and with it tea drinking and vegetarian principles. For Chinese and Japanese Zen Buddhist monks, drinking tea aided both digestion and mental discipline.

The 9th century saw a period of rich cultural development known as the Heian Age. Food was still kept simple and natural, but there was an increasing emphasis on beautiful presentation.

The ascetic tea rites of the monks were refined to an art form in the late 16th century, becoming known as the tea ceremony (cha-no-yu). The spiritual symbolism and intricate rules of 'the Way of Tea' are still observed today.

Portuguese traders were the first westerners to make contact with Japan and they introduced various new commodities, foods and practices. Over the past 400 years, western culture has continued to influence Japan both industrially and culturally, but Japanese cuisine has largely maintained its own traditions and integrity.

Flavours & Features of Japanese Food

The simplicity and elegance of Japanese cuisine lies in the subtle combining of a few essential flavourings with high-quality fresh ingredients. Reflecting the fact that Japanese food is designed to echo nature, the preference for cooking with seasonal produce influences the choice and preparation of dishes. Garnishes are arranged artistically to complement each dish, perhaps suggesting the time of year or the source of the main ingredient – it may, for example, be an autumn leaf from the area where the mushrooms were gathered.

A formal Japanese meal is a culinary tour of cooking techniques and beautiful presentation. The meal begins with tasty delicacies made with seasonal vegetables, followed by a clear soup. The pinnacle of the meal is the sashimi (raw fish) course, and after that is either a hot-pot dish or a selection of grilled, steamed, simmered and deep-fried dishes. A salad dressed with vinegar follows to cleanse the palate. Next is a bowl of rice, pickles and miso (served together) – a traditional course that serves as a reminder of frugal times in Japan's history. The meal finishes with tea and fresh fruit.

At home a meal often starts with something light, such as a miso or clear soup. The main course centres around rice – always included – and a protein dish such as fish, meat or beans. This is accompanied with vegetables and another starch dish, such as potatoes or noodles. For dessert, fruit may be offered and tea served.

Both sea and land provide the ingredients of Japanese cuisine. Among the abundant fish, shellfish and seaweeds are bonito (katsuo) and kelp (kombu), which are the basis of dashi stock (the foundation of most soups and simmered dishes). Soy beans are a prime ingredient, the versatile and nutritious bean being found, in one of its many forms (such as soy sauce, soy milk, oil, tofu or miso), in nearly every Japanese dish. Rice is the staple crop in Japan, the symbol of nourishment and the base around which a meal is created.

Sake, a wine served warm, chilled or at room temperature, is made from naturally fermented rice. The sake used for cooking is a less refined form. Mirin, another product made from rice, is a sweet rice wine with a low alcohol content, specifically manufactured for use in cooking.

The cooking process is seen as the means of imbuing a fresh ingredient with the essential seasonings of dashi, soy sauce, sake and mirin. Every technique – grilling, frying, simmering, steaming, dressing – is intended to maintain the freshness and flavour of each element in the final dish. In addition, ingredients are prepared and presented always with an emphasis on visual appeal. The cutting of ingredients is done with attention to how

they will be used in the finished dish – pieces easy to handle with chopsticks, chunks that will cook evenly in a hotpot, or fine slivers for a salad that will be coated in dressing.

Unlike in the west, where several flavours are commonly blended in one dish or on one plate, the Japanese retain the individuality of the elements in a meal. Japanese food is usually served in small portions in individual dishes, each of which is specifically chosen to highlight the food placed in it.

In Japan, green tea is prepared at any time of day and is served with most meals. It comes in different grades, according to the use: bancha, an all-purpose tea, is prepared hot or chilled; sencha is a higher-grade variety, reserved for special occasions; gyrkuro is the finest tea, the leaf used in powdered form (matcha) for the tea ceremony. The formal tea ceremony is graceful and intricate, matcha being whisked into hot water using a handmade bamboo whisk (called a chasen). Each technique, each step of the preparation and serving, has artistic and spiritual merit – a reflection of the Japanese approach to food and life.

Kitchen Equipment

CHOPSTICKS (HASHI or OTEMOTO)

These are integral not only to Japanese dining, but also to cooking. Unlike Chinese chopsticks, which have blunt ends, Japanese chopsticks taper to a point. Kitchen chopsticks are generally made of bamboo and are longer than those used for eating: they make ideal tools for picking up, mixing and flipping ingredients – all done with a delicate motion. Chopsticks for the table are traditionally made of lacquered wood. Etiquette dictates that chopsticks are never laid flat during a meal but should be rested on holders with the points supported and facing left.

GRATER (SHOGA OROSHI)

Japanese graters, used for ginger, wasabi, garlic and daikon, are usually made of ceramic or metal and come in different sizes. They are available from Asian food stores and good cookware stores. Unlike its western counterpart, a Japanese grater has teeth rather than perforations, so the flesh of the ingredient is pulped rather than cut.

KNIVES (HOCHO)

Japanese cooks use various techniques for cutting and slicing ingredients, which directly affect the way food looks and tastes. Japanese knives are renowned for their quality and are available in a range of different shapes, weights and sizes suited to particular applications. The most common is the kitchen 'carving knife' (debabocho), about 30 cm (12 in) long, used for cutting meat and fish. For cutting vegetables, a smaller, square-ended knife known as nakiri-bocho is used in most Japanese households.

DROP-LIDS (OTOSHI-BUTA)

These are round lids traditionally used when simmering food. The lid, usually made of lightweight wood, fits inside the pan and sits directly on the ingredients, keeping them immersed as they simmer and ensuring even cooking. As a substitute, you can use a circle of baking paper, or a saucepan lid that's smaller than the pan you're cooking in.

MORTAR (SURIBACHI) & PESTLE

The direct translation of the Japanese word suribachi is grinding bowl. The glazed inner surface of the ceramic bowl is scored with tiny grooves, which act like a grater when the pestle (usually made of wood) is applied to crush the ingredients. Available from Asian food stores in various sizes, they are commonly used for grinding sesame seeds, nuts or herbs.

JAPANESE OMELETTE PAN (MAKIYAKI-NABE)

This is a small, square or rectangular pan traditionally used for making the rolled omelette dashimaki. These pans are available in Asian stores, but you can substitute a good-quality omelette pan and then square off the edges of the omelette after cooking.

Sushi & Sashimi

Sushi originated around the 17th century as a slice of raw fish draped over a ball of lightly vinegared rice. Today it comes in many guises, still based on vinegared rice but using a variety of ingredients. Sushi makes a healthy snack and is very popular throughout the world. It is easy to prepare at home after a few practice runs with the sushi mat, and can easily be modified to suit individual tastes. When working with sushi rice, use wet hands to prevent sticking (have a bowl of water on the work surface).

In Japan the preparation of sashimi (sliced raw fish) displays the skills and expertise of a chef. Knife skills and selection of the perfect fresh fish are paramount. Sashimi-grade fish is available from good fishmongers.

Japanese soy sauce is the main condiment for sushi and sashimi, along with wasabi paste and pickled ginger.

‹ Sushi Pouch (page 14)

Sushi Pouch

Chakin-zushi

Makes 6

2 cups prepared sushi rice
   (page 231)

1 teaspoon finely chopped
   pickled ginger (page 230)

¼ Lebanese cucumber,
   deseeded and diced

1 tablespoon cooked peas

6 Japanese omelettes
   (page 242)

6 chives (or 6 stalks parsley)

6 small cooked prawns,
   shelled and deveined

1 teaspoon black sesame seeds,
   toasted

Combine the sushi rice, pickled ginger, cucumber and peas in a bowl. Divide the rice mixture into six portions and mould into balls.

Lay one omelette out flat on a work surface. Put a ball of rice in the centre, then bring the sides of the omelette up to form a pouch. Place a length of chive or a parsley stalk around the 'neck' of the pouch like a drawstring, tighten, and then tie. Sit a prawn on top of the pouch opening and sprinkle with sesame seeds.

Repeat with the remaining omelettes and rice mixture. Serve immediately.

Scattered Sushi

Chirashi zushi

Serves 4 as a main

- 2 tablespoons white sesame seeds, toasted
- 1 quantity prepared sushi rice (page 231)
- ½ quantity simmered shiitake mushrooms (page 65), finely sliced
- ⅓ cup (90 g/3 oz) canned bamboo shoots, drained and finely sliced
- 1 medium-sized carrot, finely sliced
- 1 Lebanese cucumber, finely sliced
- 3 Japanese omelettes (page 242), cut into thin strips
- 120 g (4 oz) sashimi-grade salmon, thinly sliced
- 1 cup snow-pea shoots
- 2 tablespoons salmon roe (optional)
- 2 sheets toasted nori (seaweed), cut into 2-cm (½-in) strips, for garnish (optional)
- 2 tablespoons sliced pickled ginger (page 230), to serve

Using a spatula or wooden rice paddle, stir sesame seeds through the sushi rice. Spread the rice over the base of a large shallow serving bowl.

Scatter the mushrooms and other sliced vegetables over the rice, then scatter with the omelette strips, salmon slices, snow-pea shoots and salmon roe (if using). Garnish with nori strips if desired. Serve immediately, accompanied with pickled ginger.

❀ You can substitute 12 cooked prawns for the roe.

Sushi Rice Rolled in Seaweed

Nori-maki

Makes 24

4 sheets toasted nori (seaweed)

1 quantity prepared sushi rice
(page 231)

wasabi paste, to taste

FILLINGS (CHOOSE ONE):

Pickled vegetables
(oshinko maki)

4 × 12-cm (5-in) strips kanpyo
or pickled cucumber

an 8-cm (3-in) length pickled
daikon, cut into thin strips

120 g (4 oz) firm tofu, cut into
1-cm × 8-cm (⅜-in × 3-in)
strips

Raw tuna (tekka maki)

200 g (7 oz) sashimi-grade
tuna, cut into 1-cm × 8-cm
(⅜-in × 3-in) strips

Cucumber roll (kappa maki)

1 Lebanese cucumber,
halved lengthways

TO SERVE

Japanese soy sauce

wasabi paste

pickled ginger (page 230)

You will need a bamboo sushi mat, for rolling.

Lay the bamboo mat on a work surface with bamboo sticks running horizontally. Top with a nori sheet, shiny side down, starting about 4 cm (1½ in) in from the edge of the mat. Using wet hands (to prevent the rice sticking to your fingers), gently press a quarter of the rice over the nori to cover evenly.

Smear a little wasabi paste in a line on the rice, about 5 cm (2 in) in from the edge closest to you.

Divide your chosen filling into four portions. (If making the pickled vegetable filling, combine all the ingredients first.) Arrange one portion in a row on top of the wasabi paste and across the width of the nori. Using both hands (wet), hold the filling in place with your fingers, then use your thumbs to draw up the bamboo mat and bring the nori sheet over the top of the filling. Press down gently but firmly, to form a cylinder. Continue the rolling process, pulling back the edge of the bamboo mat after each turn, until a neat firm roll is formed. Dab edge with a little water to seal.

Remove the mat and transfer the sushi roll to a cutting board. Repeat the process with the remaining ingredients to make another three rolls.

Using a sharp knife, cut each roll into six even slices. Place cut side up on a platter and serve with a selection of small bowls filled with the condiments.

* Bamboo sushi mats (often sold in a set with a wooden rice paddle) are available from Asian food stores and often from supermarkets.
* Ingredients such as kanpyo (dried gourd) and individual pickled vegetables are also available at Asian food stores.

Omelette Sushi

Kobana-maki

Makes 18

3 sheets toasted nori (seaweed)

3 Japanese omelettes (page 242), cooled

½ quantity prepared sushi rice (page 231)

wasabi paste, to taste

1 Lebanese cucumber, cut in half lengthways, then cut into thin strips

an 8-cm (3-in) length pickled daikon, cut into thin strips

Japanese soy sauce and pickled ginger (page 230), to serve

You will need a bamboo sushi mat, for rolling.

Lay the bamboo mat on a work surface with the bamboo sticks running horizontally. Top with a nori sheet, shiny side down, starting about 4 cm (1½ in) in from the edge of the mat. Lay an omelette over the nori.

Using wet hands (to prevent the rice sticking to your fingers), gently press a third of the rice over the omelette to cover evenly. Smear a little wasabi paste in a line on the rice, about 5 cm (2 in) in from the edge closest to you. Divide the strips of cucumber and pickled daikon each into three portions. Arrange one portion of cucumber and daikon in a row on top of the wasabi paste and across the width of the nori. >

Using both hands (wet), hold the filling in place with your fingers, then use your thumbs to draw up the bamboo mat and bring the nori sheet over the top of the filling. Press down gently but firmly, to form a cylinder. Continue the rolling process, pulling back the edge of the bamboo mat after each turn, until a neat firm roll is formed. Dab edge with a little water to seal.

Remove the mat and transfer the sushi roll to a cutting board. Repeat the process with the remaining ingredients to make another two rolls.

Using a sharp knife, cut each roll into six even slices. Place cut side up on a platter and serve with soy sauce for dipping and some pickled ginger, if desired.

Moulded Sushi

Nigiri-zushi

Makes 24

12 cooked (equal-sized) prawns, shelled and deveined but tails left intact

1 quantity prepared sushi rice (page 231)

1 piece sashimi-grade tuna or salmon, cut into 12 × 1-cm (⅜-in) strips

wasabi paste, to taste

Japanese soy sauce and pickled ginger (page 230), to serve

Carefully slit along the underside of each prawn, without cutting through the other side. Open out, and gently press to flatten (butterfly). Set aside.

Take a heaped tablespoon of rice and use wet hands to form it into a rectangle about 5 cm (2 in) long and 2 cm (¾ in) wide. Place a slice of fish in your left hand and smear a little wasabi over the top. Cup your hand and place the shaped rice on the fish, using the fingers of your right hand to mould the fish around the rice, pressing gently to form a neat oblong. Transfer to a serving plate, rice side down, and cover with a clean damp tea towel or cling wrap. Repeat the process with the remaining rice and fish, and the prawns. With the prawns, mould the rice into the opened-out prawn and leave the tail hanging off one end.

Serve accompanied with soy sauce for dipping, and some pickled ginger.

❀ Make sure each slice of fish is slightly larger than the moulded rice.

Sushi Rice in Tofu Pouches

Inari-zushi

Makes 12

6 sheets deep-fried tofu (aburage)

½ quantity prepared sushi rice (page 231)

2 tablespoons white sesame seeds, toasted

Japanese soy sauce and pickled ginger (page 230), to serve

Drain any excess liquid from the tofu sheets. Carefully slide a finger along the slit side of one sheet and open gently to form a pocket. Fill pocket with a golfball-sized mound of rice. Sprinkle the rice with toasted sesame seeds, then fold over edges of tofu sheet to enclose. Repeat the process with the remaining ingredients.

Place the filled pouches, join side down, on a serving plate. Serve with soy sauce and pickled ginger.

✿ Aburage are deep-fried sheets of tofu, available at Asian grocers. This tofu can be added to soups, simmered dishes and stir-fries.

Sushi Cones

Temaki-zushi

Makes 16

8 sheets toasted nori (seaweed)

1 Lebanese cucumber, cut in half crossways

2 cups prepared sushi rice (page 231)

wasabi paste, to taste

2 teaspoons white sesame seeds, toasted

1 avocado, halved, peeled and flesh sliced lengthways into 16 slices

2 tablespoons salmon roe, for garnish (optional)

pickled ginger (page 230), to serve

Cut nori sheets in half. Cut each cucumber half into eight long sticks.

To form a cone, place a piece of nori in the palm of your left hand (shiny side down). Wet your right hand and place about ¼ cup of the sushi rice on the nori and spread it diagonally to cover one-third of the sheet, to the left-hand side, leaving a border all around. Spread a little wasabi over the rice and sprinkle some sesame seeds on top. Place a cucumber strip and two avocado slices diagonally across the rice, pointing to the left-hand corner of the nori sheet.

Starting from the corner closest to you, draw the nori up over the filling at an angle, to produce a cone shape. Fold over the edges at the bottom of the cone, then continue rolling until filling is completely enclosed. Dab edges with a little water to seal.

Repeat process with the remaining ingredients. Top each cone with some salmon roe, if using, and serve with pickled ginger alongside.

- Other filling suggestions include cooked prawns, asparagus, simmered mushrooms (page 65), smoked salmon, pickled daikon, or omelette roll (page 244) cut into strips.

- These sushi cones are ideal for entertaining, as they are easy to prepare and guests can make their own from a selection of fillings.

Garfish in a Plum Dressing

Sayori

Serves 4 as a starter

4 medium-sized sashimi-grade
garfish, filleted and skin
removed

1½ tablespoons bainiki
(plum paste)

1 tablespoon (20 ml/¾ fl oz)
mirin (sweet cooking wine)

1 teaspoon Japanese soy sauce

a 4-cm (1½-in) piece daikon,
peeled and grated or
shredded

1 tablespoon chopped shiso
(beefsteak plant) leaves,
for garnish

Pat garfish fillets dry with paper towel.

To prepare the dressing, combine the bainiki, mirin and soy in a bowl.
Add the garfish fillets and stir to coat well. Set aside for 10 minutes.

Remove fish from marinade. Roll each fillet into a spiral, with side that's
had skin removed facing out. Place each spiral on a small serving dish and
drizzle any remaining dressing over. Serve with daikon and garnish with
a sprinkling of shiso.

❁ If shiso leaves are unavailable, use basil leaves instead. If you cannot
find bainiki, replace with mashed umeboshi (pickled plums).

Squid Rolls

Ika

Makes 8

2 small (100 g/3½ oz) sashimi-grade squid tubes, cleaned

1 sheet toasted nori (seaweed)

½ teaspoon wasabi paste

2 tablespoons pickled ginger (page 230)

a 4-cm (1½-in) piece Lebanese cucumber, halved lengthways and then sliced into 4 equal lengths

a 5-cm (2-in) piece daikon, peeled and finely shredded

Cut each squid tube in half along the sides to make two flat fillets. Cut each fillet in half lengthways. Place on a clean work surface, inner side facing upwards.

Cut the seaweed into eight equal-sized rectangles. Lay a piece of seaweed on top of a piece of squid. Working at the widest end of the squid piece, spread a little wasabi over the nori, 1 cm (⅜ in) in from the edge.

Divide the pickled ginger into eight portions and scatter one portion over the wasabi, then lay a piece of cucumber across, on top. Starting from the wide end, carefully roll up the squid piece, enclosing the filling as you go. Repeat process with remaining ingredients to make eight rolls.

If you're not eating the squid rolls immediately, cover with plastic wrap and refrigerate for up to 2 hours. Serve garnished with the shredded daikon.

Sashimi

Serves 4

450 g (1 lb) sashimi-grade salmon, tuna or trout

1 daikon, peeled and finely shredded

TO SERVE

Japanese soy sauce

pickled ginger (page 230)

wasabi paste

Choose a single variety of fish, or use a selection. Make sure the fish is thoroughly cleaned, and trim off any skin, dark flesh or blood lines. Cut flesh into 1-cm (⅜-in) slices.

On one large plate or four small ones, arrange the fish slices, overlapping slightly, in a line or a rosette pattern. Place a mound of shredded daikon alongside.

Serve with small dishes of soy sauce, pickled ginger and wasabi paste. Diners mix some wasabi into the soy, to taste, then dip the fish into the sauce. The ginger refreshes the palate.

⚜ Fish for sashimi is generally sold filleted and in lengths ready to slice. 'Sashimi-grade' fish should be super-fresh; check with your fishmonger.

⚜ Other dipping sauces that can be offered with sashimi include: combination soy sauce (page 236), ginger soy (soy sauce with a little ginger juice), and sesame soy (soy sauce with a dash of mirin and some freshly toasted sesame seeds).

Stocks & Soups

Soups play a significant role in Japanese cuisine. Miso soup is popular at breakfast time but can also be enjoyed during the day. Clear soup, known as suimono, is served between courses to refresh the palate or as a light meal with rice. (It is traditionally served in a lacquer bowl with a lid to hold the heat in.) Thick broths called shiumono are hearty and almost stew-like.

Dashi, flavoured with konbu and bonito, is the basic stock, and is one of the key ingredients in Japanese soups (and cooking in general). Starting with a quality dashi is essential, and all the other ingredients must balance and complement each other in flavour, texture and appearance.

< Dashi Stock I (page 34)

Dashi Stock I (Basic Dashi)

Ichiban dashi

Makes about 1 L (34 fl oz)

**a 10-cm (4-in) length of
kombu (kelp)**

**1½ cups (30 g/1 oz) dried
bonito flakes**

Place 1.5 L (3 pt 3 fl oz) cold water and the kombu in a large saucepan over medium–high heat. Just before water comes to the boil, remove the kombu (reserve it to make dashi stock II – page 35).

Bring water back to the boil, then quickly add ¼ cup (60 ml/3 fl oz) cold water to reduce the temperature quickly. Add the bonito flakes, increase the heat and return to a rapid boil, then remove from the heat immediately.

Allow the bonito flakes to settle and sink to the bottom of the saucepan. Strain the liquid through a fine mesh sieve lined with muslin (reserve the bonito flakes to make dashi stock II).

❀ You can store the reserved kombu and bonito flakes, separately, in sealed containers in the refrigerator for 2–3 days.

❀ Do not allow the stock to boil with the kombu in it, or to boil for longer than 2–3 seconds when the bonito flakes are added, as it will become bitter.

Dashi Stock II (Secondary Dashi)

Niban dashi

Makes about 3 cups (750 ml/25 fl oz)

kombu (kelp) and bonito flakes
  reserved from dashi stock I
  (page 34)

extra ¾ cup (15 g/½ oz) dried
  bonito flakes

Place 1.5 L (3 pt 3 fl oz) cold water in a saucepan and add the reserved kombu and bonito flakes. Bring to the boil over high heat, then immediately reduce heat to low and simmer for 20 minutes or until stock is reduced by half. Remove from heat and sprinkle the extra bonito flakes over. Allow the flakes to settle to the bottom, then strain the stock through a muslin-lined strainer. Discard the kombu and bonito flakes.

❀ Basic dashi has a fresh, refined and distinctive 'Japanese' flavour that is used for soups. Secondary dashi has a stronger flavour and is mainly used for stews and noodle dishes.

Miso Soup

Miso-shiru

Serves 4

3½ cups (875 ml/29½ fl oz)
  dashi stock II (page 35)

100 g (3½ oz) red miso paste

250 g (9 oz) firm silken tofu,
  drained and cut into 1.5-cm
  (⅝-in) cubes

4 tablespoons finely sliced
  spring onions, for garnish

sansho pepper (optional)

Place ¼ cup (60 ml/2 fl oz) of the dashi in a small bowl, add the miso paste and blend until smooth.

Place remaining dashi in a medium-sized saucepan over medium–high heat and bring just to the boil, then reduce to a low simmer. Spoon the miso mixture into the simmering stock, stirring continuously to dissolve the miso paste. Place the tofu in the stock and cook for a minute until heated through.

Ladle soup into four bowls. Scatter with the spring onions and sprinkle with sansho pepper, if using. Serve immediately.

Miso Vegetable Soup

Satsuma-jiru

Serves 4

1 L (34 fl oz) dashi stock I
(page 34)

100 g (3½ oz) white miso paste

1 carrot, cut into quarters
lengthways, then thinly
sliced

1 medium-sized daikon, peeled,
cut into quarters lengthways,
then thinly sliced

1 sweet potato, sliced into
thin rounds

4 fresh shiitake mushrooms,
stems discarded and caps
sliced

1 spring onion, finely sliced,
for garnish

Place ½ cup (125 ml/4 fl oz) of the dashi in a small bowl, add the miso paste and blend until smooth. Set aside.

Bring the remaining dashi to a simmer in a large saucepan over medium–high heat. Add the carrot and cook for 3 minutes, then add the daikon, sweet potato and mushrooms, and simmer for another 3 minutes. When the vegetables are just tender, stir in the diluted miso paste until well combined.

Serve immediately, in small deep bowls, sprinkled with spring onion.

❀ Other vegetables can be substituted. Try fresh enoki mushrooms, bamboo shoots, and spinach or chrysanthemum leaves (available at Asian food stores).

Soy Bean & Ginger Soup

Serves 4

6 spring onions, white parts
finely chopped and green
parts reserved

750 g (1 lb 10 oz) fresh or
frozen soy beans in the pod
(edamame)

1 tablespoon (20 ml/¾ fl oz)
vegetable oil

2 teaspoons sesame oil

2 teaspoons grated fresh
ginger

1 clove garlic, crushed

1 L (34 fl oz) chicken stock

salt and ground white pepper

Japanese soy sauce, to serve

Cut the reserved spring-onion greens into thin strips 5 cm (2 in) long. Place in a bowl of iced water and set aside in the fridge while you prepare the soup (the chilled water will make the strips curl).

Bring a large saucepan of water to the boil. Add the soy beans, return to the boil and cook for 5 minutes. Drain beans, then plunge them at once into a large bowl of cold water so that they cool instantly. Squeeze each pod to pop out the beans, and place in a bowl (discard the pods).

Heat the oils in a large, heavy-based saucepan over medium heat. Add the spring-onion whites and cook for 3 minutes to soften, being careful not to let them colour. Stir in the ginger and garlic, and cook for 30 seconds. >

Add the stock and beans, increase the heat and bring to the boil. Reduce heat to a simmer and cook for 15 minutes or until beans are tender.

Purée soup until smooth, using a hand-held blender or food processor. Return to a clean saucepan over low heat and season with salt and white pepper.

Ladle soup into bowls and garnish with the drained spring-onion curls. Pass around the soy sauce to drizzle over, if desired.

Pumpkin, Wakame & Tofu Soup

Serves 4 as a starter or light meal

2 teaspoons dried wakame (seaweed) pieces

1 L (34 fl oz) dashi stock II (page 35)

200 g (8 oz) pumpkin, peeled and cut into 1-cm (⅜-in) cubes

200 g (7 oz) firm silken tofu, cut into 1-cm (⅜-in) cubes

3 tablespoons white miso paste

⅓ cup radish sprouts, for garnish

Soak the wakame pieces in a bowl of water for 5 minutes or until just soft. Drain well.

Bring the dashi to the boil in a saucepan over medium–high heat. Add the pumpkin and cook for 8–10 minutes, or until just tender but not mushy.

Using a slotted spoon, remove the pumpkin and divide between warmed bowls, and top with the tofu.

Add the miso and drained wakame to the stock and bring to a simmer, stirring until the miso is dissolved. Ladle soup over the pumpkin and tofu, garnish with the radish sprouts and serve immediately.

Clear Fish Soup

Sumashi-jiru

Serves 4

1 L (34 fl oz) dashi stock I
(page 34)

½ teaspoon Japanese soy sauce

1 teaspoon sake (Japanese rice
wine)

¼–½ teaspoon salt

a 2-cm (¾-in) piece daikon,
peeled

4 button mushrooms

3 tablespoons (45 g/1½ oz)
cornflour

2 × 90-g (3-oz) white fish
fillets (John Dory, snapper,
blue eye)

8 leaves shiso (beefsteak
plant) or mitsuba (Japanese
parsley), for garnish

4 thin strips lemon zest,
for garnish

Bring the dashi to a simmer in a saucepan over medium heat. Reduce heat to low, then add the soy, sake and salt to taste, adjusting seasoning if needed. Keep hot.

Using a vegetable peeler or small sharp knife, peel strips from around the circumference of the daikon, to make curls.

Trim the stems from the mushrooms and discard. Wipe mushroom caps with a damp cloth, then roll them in half the cornflour to coat, shaking off any excess. Cut each fish fillet into two even-sized pieces and coat in the remaining cornflour, shaking off the excess. >

Bring a saucepan of lightly salted water to the boil. Add the mushrooms, return to the boil and cook for 3 minutes. Remove with a slotted spoon and transfer one to each of four soup bowls.

Add the fish to the saucepan and simmer for 3 minutes or until just cooked. Remove with a slotted spoon and transfer each piece to a soup bowl.

Divide the daikon curls between the soup bowls. Pour the hot stock over, garnish with shiso or mitsuba leaves and lemon zest, and serve immediately.

Rice Broth

Zosui

Serves 4

2 dried shiitake mushrooms, soaked in ½ cup (125 ml/ 4 fl oz) hot water for 30 minutes

3 cups (750 ml/25 fl oz) dashi stock II (page 35)

1 skinless chicken breast fillet, cut crossways into thin slices

1½ cups basic steamed rice (page 233)

2 teaspoons Japanese soy sauce

12 baby spinach leaves

1 egg, lightly beaten

1½ teaspoons ginger juice (see note on page 47)

a 2-cm (¾-in) piece fresh ginger, cut into 12 very fine slices, for garnish

Drain the mushrooms and reserve the liquid. Discard mushroom stalks and slice the caps finely, then return to the soaking liquid and set aside.

Bring the dashi to the boil in a large saucepan over high heat, then reduce heat immediately to a gentle simmer.

Meanwhile, half-fill a medium-sized saucepan with water and bring to the boil. Add the sliced chicken and cook for 45 seconds, then remove from the heat and drain. Add the chicken, the mushrooms and their soaking liquid to the simmering stock, and cook for 10 minutes. >

Rinse the cooked rice under running water, then drain. Stir the rice and soy sauce into the stock, combining well, then bring back to a simmer. Using chopsticks, stir in the spinach leaves and beaten egg. Cover pan with a lid for 30 seconds until egg is only just cooked and spinach wilted.

Stir in the ginger juice and ladle soup immediately into deep bowls. Scatter with sliced fresh ginger, and serve.

Ginger juice is useful for sauces and other dishes where you want the flavour, but not the texture, of ginger. To make 1 teaspoon of juice, grate a 3-cm (1¼-in) piece of fresh ginger on a Japanese ceramic grater over a small bowl. Squeeze the grated ginger to release as much juice as possible, and discard the pulp. (Note: the older the ginger, the larger the piece needed to produce the amount of juice required.)

Pork & Miso Soup

Tonjiru

Serves 4 as a light meal

100 g (3½ oz) konnyaku, cut
into 1.5-cm (⅝-in) dice

120 g (4 oz) burdock root, skin
scraped with a sharp knife

1 L (34 fl oz) dashi stock II
(page 35)

100 g (3½ oz) white or red
miso paste

1 tablespoon (20 ml/¾ fl oz)
vegetable oil

250 g (9 oz) boneless pork belly,
cut into 2.5-cm (1-in) cubes

150 g (5 oz) taro, peeled and
cut into 2-cm (¾-in) cubes

1 carrot, halved lengthways
and then cut into 1-cm
(⅜-in) slices

a 5-cm (2-in) piece daikon,
peeled and sliced thinly
lengthways

2 spring onions (white parts
only), thinly sliced

Bring a small saucepan of water to the boil. Add the konnyaku and boil for
1 minute. Drain well.

Using a vegetable peeler, shave the burdock root lengthways into thin
strips. Place strips in a bowl of cold water and leave to soak for 10 minutes
to remove any bitterness. Drain well, rinse and drain again.

Transfer ½ cup (125 ml/4 fl oz) dashi to a small bowl. Add the miso paste
and blend until smooth. Set aside.

Heat oil in a non-stick frying pan over medium–high heat and add pork. Cook for 5 minutes to lightly brown all sides of the pork pieces. Remove and drain on paper towel.

Meanwhile, bring the remaining dashi to a simmer in a large saucepan over a medium–high heat. Add the pork, taro, carrot, daikon and konnyaku, and return to the boil. Reduce heat to a simmer and cook for 45–60 minutes, skimming the surface to remove any rising scum. When the pork is cooked through and vegetables are tender, stir in the diluted miso paste until dissolved and well combined.

Ladle soup into bowls and sprinkle with the sliced spring onions. Serve immediately.

❁ Konnyaku, taro and burdock root are available from Asian food stores. You can substitute potatoes for the taro.

Vegetables
& Salads

Vegetable dishes generally constitute the main part of a Japanese meal. Even though many vegetables are available year-round, the cuisine is shaped by the seasons and what is available locally. Autumn brings mushrooms and chestnuts, while in winter hotpots and stews include potato, cabbage and pickled vegetables. Japanese greens are favoured in spring, and in summer dishes such as grated fresh vegetables and cold noodles with cucumber are refreshing.

There are two main styles of salad popular in Japan: sunomono, with vinegar-based dressings; and ae-mono, with thicker dressings that include either sesame seeds, tofu or miso. The dressings are used with salads of raw or cooked vegetables or seafood.

Japanese salads are served in small portions, often at the start of a meal or near the end (before rice). You will find more salad recipes in the Noodle & Rice Dishes section.

‹ Spinach Rolls with a Sesame Dressing (page 52)

Spinach Rolls with a Sesame Dressing

Serves 4 as a side dish

450 g (1 lb) spinach, stems discarded

1 tablespoon toasted white or black sesame seeds, for garnish

DRESSING

⅓ cup white sesame seeds, lightly toasted

1 teaspoon sugar

2 teaspoons Japanese soy sauce

2 tablespoons (40 ml/1½ fl oz) dashi stock II (page 35)

Bring a medium-sized saucepan of lightly salted water to the boil. Add the spinach leaves and cook for 45 seconds. Drain, then plunge spinach into a bowl of iced water to halt the cooking process. Drain again and squeeze out any excess moisture until you have a solid mound.

For the dressing, place sesame seeds in a suribachi or mortar, and grind until coarsely crushed. Add sugar, soy and dashi, stirring with the pestle to form a paste. Combine with the spinach in a bowl and mix well.

Transfer spinach to a bamboo sushi mat and spread along one edge of the mat to form a log about 10 cm (4 in) in length. Use the bamboo mat to roll spinach into a cylinder, pressing gently to pack it firmly. Cut spinach roll into four even pieces and dip one end of each portion into sesame seeds. Arrange on a serving plate, sesame seeds facing up.

Grilled Eggplant

Yakinasu

Serves 4 as a starter or side dish

8 Asian eggplants

vegetable oil for brushing

3 teaspoons ginger juice
(see note page 47)

Japanese soy sauce, to serve

1 lime or lemon,
cut into wedges

Preheat a grill pan or barbecue grill to high.

Brush the eggplants lightly with oil. Prick several times all over with a skewer, place on preheated grill and cook, turning frequently, until the skin wrinkles and becomes very dark (10–15 minutes, depending on the grill temperature and the size of the eggplants).

Plunge the cooked eggplants into a bowl of cold water to stop the cooking process. Drain well, then pull away and discard the skin. Arrange the whole eggplants on a platter or individual plates.

Serve at room temperature, drizzled with a little ginger juice and soy sauce. Offer lime or lemon wedges, for squeezing.

❁ Asian eggplants (sometimes called Japanese or Chinese eggplants) are a long, slender variety with tender skin and a delicate flavour. They don't need salting or peeling before cooking.

Simmered Burdock Root

Serves 4 as a side dish

250 g (9 oz) burdock root, peeled

1 tablespoon (20 ml/¾ fl oz) vegetable oil

1 teaspoon sesame oil

2 tablespoons (40 ml/1½ fl oz) Japanese soy sauce

2 tablespoons (40 ml/1½ fl oz) mirin (sweet cooking wine)

1 tablespoon (20 ml/¾ fl oz) sake (Japanese rice wine)

2 teaspoons caster sugar

Cut the burdock root into matchsticks. Place in a bowl and cover with cold water for 10 minutes (this helps remove any bitterness). Drain, and pat dry with paper towel.

Heat the oils in a non-stick frying pan over medium heat. Add the burdock and stir-fry for 8–10 minutes until lightly golden. Add the remaining ingredients and stir to dissolve sugar and mix ingredients well. Cook until burdock is tender and the liquid has evaporated (10–15 minutes).

Serve this dish hot or at room temperature, as an accompaniment to simmered fish dishes or grilled meats.

Asparagus with a Japanese-style Hollandaise Sauce

Serves 4 as a side dish or starter

16 thick spears asparagus, cut into 5-cm (2-in) lengths

shichimi togarashi (seven-spice mix), for garnish (optional)

SAUCE

3 egg yolks

3 teaspoons Japanese soy sauce

½ teaspoon Japanese mustard (optional)

1 teaspoon caster sugar

1½ tablespoons dashi stock II (page 35)

3 tablespoons (60 ml/2 fl oz) Japanese rice vinegar

Cook asparagus for 1–2 minutes in a saucepan of boiling salted water, until just tender. Remove from pan and plunge into a bowl of iced water to stop the cooking process. Drain well.

Place all the sauce ingredients in a medium-sized heatproof bowl and whisk to combine. Place the bowl over a pan of simmering water and continue to stir for 3–5 minutes or until the sauce thickens enough to coat the back of a spoon.

Arrange the asparagus on serving plates with a small bowl of the sauce alongside, for dipping. If desired, sprinkle asparagus with shichimi.

Soy-grilled Baby Corn

Serves 4 as a side dish

12 cobs fresh baby corn, husks
   removed (or use 2 × 400-g/
   14-oz cans baby corn)

3 tablespoons (60 ml/2 fl oz)
   combination soy sauce
   (page 236)

2 teaspoons sesame oil

If using fresh corn, bring a medium-sized saucepan of lightly salted water to the boil. Add the corn and return water to the boil, then cook for 2 minutes. Drain well. (If using canned corn, drain, and pat dry with paper towel.)

Preheat griller or barbecue grill to hot.

Place corn, combination soy sauce and sesame oil in a bowl and toss to coat corn well. Remove corn, letting any excess marinade drain back into the bowl, then place cobs directly on the barbecue or (on a baking tray lined with aluminium foil) under the griller. Cook for about 3 minutes, turning frequently and basting with the marinade, until the kernels are turning golden brown.

Serve hot, with any leftover marinade in a bowl for dipping.

Eggplant with Miso

Nasu dengaku

Serves 4 as a side dish

2 medium-sized globe eggplants
(about 300 g/10½ oz each)

vegetable oil, for brushing

1 tablespoon white sesame
seeds, toasted

DENGAKU MISO

100 g (3½ oz) red or white
miso paste

2 egg yolks

2 tablespoons (30 g/1 oz)
sugar

2 tablespoons (40 ml/1½ fl oz)
mirin (sweet cooking wine)

2 tablespoons (40 ml/1½ fl oz)
sake (Japanese rice wine)

½ cup (125 ml/3½ fl oz) dashi
stock II (page 35)

To make the dengaku miso, place the miso, egg yolks, sugar, mirin and sake in a small saucepan over medium heat and stir to dissolve sugar. Add the dashi and simmer for 3–4 minutes until sauce thickens. Remove from heat and set aside.

Cut each eggplant in half lengthways. Score the surface of the flesh in a criss-cross pattern to a depth of 1 cm (⅜ in). Brush the cut surfaces and the skin generously with oil.

Heat a non-stick frying pan over medium heat and put in eggplants, cut side down. Cook for 2 minutes, until golden brown, then turn over and cook on the skin side for 2 minutes. Remove from pan and drain on paper towel. >

Preheat griller to medium–hot.

Spread the dengaku miso over the cut surface of each eggplant half, then cook under the griller for 3–4 minutes or until topping is golden. Transfer eggplant to a plate, sprinkle with sesame seeds and serve at once.

Simmered Pumpkin

Serves 4–6 as a side dish

500 g (1 lb 2 oz) Japanese
  pumpkin (kabocha)

2 cups (500 ml/17 fl oz) dashi
  stock II (page 35)

2 tablespoons (40 ml/1½ fl oz)
  Japanese soy sauce

1 tablespoon (15 g/½ oz) caster
  sugar

2 tablespoons (40 ml/1½ fl oz)
  mirin (sweet cooking wine)

Cut the unpeeled pumpkin into 5-cm (2-in) cubes. Using a vegetable peeler, remove some of the skin from each cube to round off the edges.

Combine the dashi, soy, sugar and mirin in a large saucepan and bring to the boil. Add the pumpkin pieces, skin side down, and return to the boil. Reduce the heat to a simmer, cover, and cook for 15–20 minutes or until pieces are tender and easily pierced with a knife, but not breaking up.

To serve, use a slotted spoon to transfer the pumpkin to a shallow bowl. Return pan to high heat, bring liquid to a simmer and reduce to about 1 cup (250 ml/8½ fl oz). Pour this over the pumpkin.

Sautéed Lotus Root & Carrot

Serves 4–6 as a side dish

350 g (12 oz) fresh lotus root

1 tablespoon (20 ml/¾ fl oz)
vegetable oil

1 teaspoon sesame oil

1 carrot, sliced diagonally
into thin rounds

1 tablespoon (20 ml/¾ fl oz)
sake (Japanese rice wine)

1 tablespoon (20 ml/¾ fl oz)
Japanese soy sauce

1½ tablespoons (30 ml/1 fl oz)
mirin (sweet cooking wine)

1 teaspoon white sesame seeds,
toasted

Peel lotus root and cut into 5-mm (¼-in) slices. Place in a bowl of cold water for 15 minutes (this helps get rid of any bitterness), then drain and pat dry with paper towel.

Heat the oils in a non-stick frying pan over medium–high heat. Add lotus root and carrot, toss to coat and cook for 10 minutes or until just tender. Pour in the sake and cook for about a minute, until sake has been absorbed. Add the soy and mirin, and cook for 2 minutes or until liquid is absorbed.

Transfer to a plate, sprinkle with the sesame seeds and serve warm or at room temperature.

❀ Fresh lotus root is available from Asian food stores and some produce markets. It is also available frozen or canned.

Simmered Shiitake Mushrooms

Shiitake kara-ni

Serves 6 as a side dish

8 large dried shiitake mushrooms

3 tablespoons (60 ml/2 fl oz) sake (Japanese rice wine)

3 tablespoons (60 ml/2 fl oz) Japanese soy sauce

3 tablespoons (60 ml/2 fl oz) mirin (sweet cooking wine)

Soak mushrooms in 2 cups (500 ml/17 fl oz) hot water for 30 minutes. Drain, reserving ¾ cup (180 ml/6 fl oz) of the soaking liquid. Cut off and discard stems; you can either leave the caps whole or slice them into 5-mm (¼-in) strips.

Combine the reserved soaking liquid with the sake, soy and mirin in a small saucepan. Add the mushrooms, place pan over high heat and bring to the boil. Reduce to a very low simmer and cover with a lid (leave it slightly askew). Cook for 30–40 minutes, stirring occasionally, until the liquid has almost evaporated, then remove from heat and leave to cool a little.

Serve mushrooms chilled as a condiment, at room temperature as a side dish, or sliced in sushi. The mushrooms will keep, in an airtight container in the refrigerator, for up to 2 weeks.

❀ You can use 200 g (7 oz) fresh shiitake mushrooms instead of the dried, in which case there's no need to soak them. If so, replace the reserved soaking liquid with ⅔ cup (160 ml/5½ fl oz) dashi stock II (page 35).

Japanese Coleslaw

Serves 6–8 as a side dish

150 g (5 oz) Chinese cabbage
150 g (5 oz) red cabbage
1 carrot, peeled
½ daikon, peeled

DRESSING

½ cup Japanese mayonnaise
1½ tablespoons (30 ml/1 fl oz)
    salad dressing (page 238)
¼–½ teaspoon wasabi paste

Finely shred the cabbages, and place in a large bowl. Cut the carrot and daikon into fine matchsticks (a mandoline fitted with a 5-mm/¼-in blade is best for this, but you can use a knife instead). Add to the cabbage.

Combine the dressing ingredients in a bowl and mix well, adding extra salad dressing or wasabi to taste.

Stir the dressing into the cabbage mixture to coat well, and transfer to a serving bowl.

❀ Japanese mayonnaise is richer, creamier and slightly sweeter than its western counterparts. It is available from Asian food stores.

Carrot & Daikon Salad

Kohaku namasu

Serves 6 as a side dish

1 daikon, about 20 cm (8 in) long, peeled

1 medium-sized carrot, peeled

½ teaspoon salt

⅓ cup (80 ml/3 fl oz) Japanese rice vinegar

2 tablespoons (40 ml/1½ fl oz) mirin (sweet cooking wine)

1 teaspoon caster sugar

a 4-cm (1½-in) length of kombu (kelp), wiped with a damp cloth

Using a vegetable peeler, shave the daikon lengthways into thin strips. Repeat with the carrot. Place vegetables in a glass or ceramic bowl, sprinkle with salt, toss to coat, and then set aside for 15 minutes. Pat dry with paper towel, to remove excess moisture.

Place the rice vinegar, mirin and sugar in a bowl and stir until sugar dissolves. Add the prepared vegetables and the kombu, and toss to coat in the vinegar mixture. Cover, and refrigerate overnight.

The next day, drain any excess liquid from the vegetables and discard the kombu. Serve the salad with grilled or fried dishes.

Chilled Tofu

Hiyayakko

Serves 4

300 g (10½ oz) firm silken tofu, chilled

2 teaspoons finely grated fresh ginger (reserve the juice)

2 spring onions, thinly sliced

1 tablespoon white sesame seeds, toasted

3 teaspoons dried bonito flakes

Japanese soy sauce, to serve

sesame oil, to serve

shichimi togarashi (seven-spice mix), for garnish (optional)

Drain the tofu. Carefully cut into four even-sized pieces and transfer to four shallow bowls. (Alternatively, you can serve the tofu in one piece – see note below.)

Top each piece of tofu with a small mound of grated ginger and drizzle with the juice. Sprinkle the spring onions, sesame seeds and bonito over the top, then drizzle with a little soy sauce and sesame oil. Sprinkle with shichimi togarashi, if using.

❀ The tofu can be presented in one piece, on a plate with the toppings, so guests can serve themselves.

Crab Salad

Kani sunomono

Serves 6 as a starter

3 tablespoons (60 ml/2 fl oz)
Japanese rice vinegar

⅓ cup (80 ml/3 fl oz) dashi
stock I (page 34)

1 tablespoon (20 ml/¾ fl oz)
Japanese soy sauce

3 teaspoons mirin
(sweet cooking wine)

220 g (7 oz) freshly cooked
crab meat

2 teaspoons ginger juice
(see note page 47)

First, make the dressing by combining the rice vinegar, dashi, soy and mirin in a small saucepan over high heat. Bring to the boil, then remove immediately from heat. Leave to cool to room temperature, then refrigerate until required.

Shred the crab meat finely and pile onto individual plates. Stir the ginger juice into the dressing, then spoon some over each portion of crab.

● This salad can also be served in lettuce cups, or garnished with shredded shiso leaves.

● You can substitute 12 small, cooked peeled prawns for the crab meat.

Potato Salad

Serves 6 as a side dish

500 g (1 lb 2 oz) large potatoes

1 small red onion, halved
and very thinly sliced

1 Lebanese cucumber

½ teaspoon salt

⅔ cup Japanese mayonnaise

60 g (2 oz) sliced ham
(optional)

2 hard-boiled eggs,
shelled and sliced

ground white pepper

Place potatoes in a saucepan and cover with cold water. Place saucepan over high heat, bring to the boil and cook for about 20 minutes, until potatoes are tender. Drain well. When potatoes are just cool enough to handle, peel and then place in a large bowl. Lightly crush flesh with a fork to break up a little.

Place onion slices in a bowl and cover with water. Set aside for 10 minutes (this removes any bitterness). Drain onions and pat dry with paper towel.

Cut the cucumber in half lengthways, scoop out the seeds and then cut flesh across into 5-mm (¼-in) slices. Sprinkle with the salt and leave for 2 minutes, then squeeze out any excess moisture.

Add the mayonnaise, ham, onion and cucumber to the potatoes while they're still warm, and gently mix to combine. Transfer to a platter, scatter with the sliced egg, and season with white pepper.

Grilled Shiitake Mushrooms

Yaki-shiitake ponzu-ae

Serves 4

12 fresh shiitake mushrooms, stems discarded

sea salt

vegetable oil for brushing

1 tablespoon chopped spring onions

⅓ cup (80 ml/3 fl oz) ponzu sauce (page 237)

Preheat grill pan or barbecue grill to medium–hot.

Sprinkle the mushrooms lightly with salt on both sides. Brush the grill lightly with oil, place mushrooms on it, underside down, and grill for 2 minutes. Turn mushrooms over and grill for another 2 minutes.

Stir chopped spring onions into the ponzu sauce. Place the hot mushrooms, underside up, on a platter or individual plates. Spoon the ponzu sauce over and serve immediately.

Nashi & Celery Salad

Serves 4

¼ cup walnut halves

⅓ cup Japanese mayonnaise

2 teaspoons white miso paste

1 tablespoon (20 ml/1½ fl oz) Japanese rice vinegar, or to taste

2 nashi pears

1 tablespoon (20 ml/1½ fl oz) freshly squeezed lemon juice

1 teaspoon ginger juice (see note page 47)

2 sticks celery (including leaves) from the inner section

Preheat the oven to 150°C (300°F). Spread walnuts on a baking tray and toast in the oven for 8–10 minutes, until aromatic and golden. Set aside to cool, then chop coarsely.

Combine the mayonnaise, miso and vinegar in a large bowl and mix well.

Quarter the pears, remove the cores, and cut into fine slices. Place in a bowl with the lemon juice and ginger juice, tossing to coat (this will prevent the flesh discolouring and also add flavour). Using a mandoline or a sharp knife, cut the celery sticks on the diagonal into fine slices. Chop the leaves roughly.

Drain the pear slices. Add to the mayonnaise with the celery slices, and toss gently to coat evenly. Pile salad into a dish and sprinkle with walnuts and celery leaves before serving.

Steamed Eggplant Salad

Serves 4 as a side dish

4 baby globe or Asian eggplants

1 teaspoon finely grated fresh ginger (reserve the juice)

3 tablespoons (60 ml/2 fl oz) salad dressing (page 238)

2 tablespoons chopped mitsuba (Japanese parsley) or flat-leaf parsley, for garnish

dried bonito flakes, for garnish

Remove skin from eggplants using a vegetable peeler or sharp paring knife. Place eggplants in a bowl of lightly salted cold water, set aside for 10 minutes and then drain.

Place eggplants in a steamer fitted over a saucepan of boiling water. Cover with a tight-fitting lid and steam for 8–10 minutes, until tender and cooked through. Remove eggplants, place between two plates and weigh down with cans of food. Place in the refrigerator to chill for an hour.

To serve, remove eggplants from refrigerator and pour off the excess liquid. Cut flesh into 5-cm (2-in) lengths and pile on a serving dish. Combine the ginger and its juice with the prepared dressing, then pour it over the eggplant. Sprinkle with the mitsuba leaves and bonito flakes before serving.

Cucumber & Wakame Salad

3 tablespoons (60 ml/2 fl oz)
Japanese rice vinegar

2 tablespoons (40 ml/1½ fl oz)
Japanese soy sauce

2 teaspoons caster sugar

2 tablespoons dried wakame
(seaweed), cut into pieces

2 Lebanese cucumbers

1 teaspoon salt

To make dressing, combine the vinegar, soy and sugar in a small saucepan over medium heat for 1 minute, until the sugar dissolves. Remove from heat immediately, leave to cool, then refrigerate for 20 minutes until chilled.

Soak the wakame in a large bowl of water for 5–10 minutes, until softened. Drain, rinse under cold water, drain well again, and pat dry with paper towel to remove any excess moisture.

Cut each cucumber in half lengthways and scoop out the seeds. Slice each half across into fine slices. Dissolve the salt in about 2 cups cold water, add the cucumber slices and soak for 10 minutes. Drain well, then pat dry with paper towel.

Place the cucumber and wakame in a bowl, pour the chilled dressing over, and toss gently to combine. Serve in individual bowls.

Noodle & Rice Dishes

Noodles are a popular staple in the Japanese diet. Varieties include: ramen, soba (buckwheat), shiritaki (made from konnyaku), udon (wheat) and somen (also made from wheat but much finer). Noodles have myriad uses in Japanese cuisine – added to chilled salads in summer; and appearing in soups and one-pot dishes in winter.

For centuries, rice has been the mainstay of the Japanese diet, deemed to be a gift from the Shinto deity Inari. The Japanese word for rice is gohan, meaning meal. Japanese short-grain rice is polished and translucent, and when cooked the grains stick together, making it suitable to eat with chopsticks. A bowl of rice is usually placed in a central position on the table or in front of each guest, with the other, 'secondary', dishes surrounding it.

< Somen Noodle Salad (page 80)

Somen Noodle Salad

Serves 4 as a light meal

2 Lebanese cucumbers, halved lengthways and seeds removed

a 5-cm (2-in) length daikon, peeled

1 teaspoon salt

1 tablespoon dried wakame (seaweed) flakes

4 bundles (100 g/3½ oz) somen noodles

250 g (9 oz) cooked crab meat, shredded into bite-sized pieces

3 spring onions, thinly sliced on the diagonal

10 shiso (beefsteak plant) leaves, chopped (or use 1 tablespoon each of chopped mint and basil leaves)

DRESSING

⅓ cup (80 ml/3 fl oz) Japanese rice vinegar

½ teaspoon caster sugar

2 tablespoons (40 ml/1½ fl oz) mirin

1 tablespoon (20 ml/¾ fl oz) ponzu sauce (page 237)

1 teaspoon ginger juice (see note page 47)

1 teaspoon sesame oil

Cut cucumber halves across into thin slices. Slice daikon thinly lengthways, then cut each slice across into four. Place cucumber and daikon in a colander, sprinkle with salt, then toss together, gently rubbing salt in at the same time. Leave for 15 minutes, then rinse under cold running water and drain well. Gently squeeze out excess moisture, and refrigerate until ready to use.

To make the dressing, combine all the ingredients and mix well.

Soak the wakame flakes in a few tablespoons water for about 5 minutes, until reconstituted. Drain well and refrigerate until ready to use.

Bring a large saucepan of salted water to the boil. Add the noodles and simmer for 2–3 minutes (or according to packet instructions) until cooked through and soft. Drain noodles, then rinse under cold running water to cool completely. Drain well again.

Place noodles, crab meat, cucumber, daikon, wakame and spring onions in a bowl and toss to combine. Pour the dressing over and toss again to coat ingredients. Divide mixture between serving bowls and scatter with the shiso leaves. Serve immediately.

Somen noodles are fine white wheat noodles. They are often served cold in salads, or in a light broth. They are available from Japanese grocers.

Noodle Sukiyaki

Udon suki

Serves 6

- 450 g (1 lb) dried udon noodles
- 6 Chinese cabbage leaves
- 350 g (12 oz) spinach leaves
- 1 small carrot, cut into 6 lengthways
- 6 spring onions (white parts only), cut into 5-cm (2-in) lengths
- 400 g (14 oz) firm tofu, cut into 6 pieces
- 100 g (3½ oz) konnyaku, cut into 6 slices
- 6 fresh shiitake mushrooms, stems discarded
- 100 g (3½ oz) canned bamboo shoots, drained and thinly sliced
- 450 g (1 lb) skinless chicken thigh fillets, cut into 4-cm (1½-in) pieces
- 6 raw (green) king prawns, peeled and deveined
- 250 g (9 oz) snapper fillets (or other firm white fish), cut into 6 slices
- 1 omelette roll (page 244), cut into 6 (optional)
- 1.5 L (3 pt 3 fl oz) chicken stock, plus extra if needed
- 3 tablespoons (60 ml/2 fl oz) Japanese soy sauce
- salt and ground white pepper

DIPPING SAUCE

- ⅓ cup (80 ml/3 fl oz) Japanese soy sauce
- ⅓ cup (80 ml/3 fl oz) freshly squeezed lemon juice
- 2 tablespoons finely sliced spring onions
- a 10-cm (4-in) length daikon, peeled and finely grated >

You will need a portable electric or gas hotplate for the broth, as this dish is served at the table.

Bring a large saucepan of salted water to the boil. Add the noodles, bring water back to the boil and cook for 15–20 minutes (or according to packet instructions) until noodles are only just cooked – don't overcook, as they will be cooked again in the broth later. Drain noodles and rinse under cold water to stop the cooking process. Drain well and arrange on a platter.

Immerse cabbage leaves in a saucepan of boiling salted water for 2 minutes, or until tender. Remove with tongs, plunge into a bowl of iced water to stop cooking process, then drain well. Return water to the boil and cook spinach for 1–2 minutes, until wilted. Remove from pan, plunge into a bowl of iced water, then drain well and squeeze out any excess water. Repeat this cooking and cooling process with the carrot and spring-onion pieces, cooking them for 2 minutes.

Lay a cabbage leaf flat on a work surface and place one-sixth of the spinach at the top edge of the leaf. Place a piece of carrot and spring onion on top, then roll up the leaf from the top edge downwards. Cut the cabbage roll into two. Repeat with the remaining leaves and filling.

Arrange all the prepared ingredients – cabbage rolls, tofu, konnyaku, mushrooms, bamboo, chicken, prawns, fish and omelette roll (if using) – on top of the noodles. Combine all the ingredients for the dipping sauce and then divide between six small bowls. Set aside.

Bring chicken stock to the boil in a flameproof casserole or saucepan over medium heat, then reduce to a simmer.

Transfer broth to the table, keeping it hot over the portable hotplate. Give each person their own bowl. Diners choose ingredients from the platter and cook these in the broth, using chopsticks or small mesh strainers (see note below), then dip them into the sauce.

When only the noodles are remaining on the platter, add them to the broth (with extra stock if needed) and return to the boil. Add the soy and season with salt and pepper. Cook until the noodles are heated through. Transfer noodles to serving bowls and ladle the broth over.

For cooking ingredients in the broth, you can supply guests with small mesh strainers (usually with a bamboo handle), available in Asian food stores.

Miso Ramen

Serves 4

500 g (1 lb 2 oz) fresh ramen
noodles

1.25 L (2 pt 10 fl oz) dashi
stock II (page 35)

100 g (3½ oz) red or white
miso paste

300 g (10½ oz) firm silken
tofu, cut into 8 pieces

1 tablespoon (20 ml/¾ fl oz)
vegetable oil

1 carrot, cut into matchsticks

1 clove garlic, crushed

1 teaspoon finely grated fresh
ginger

¼ Chinese cabbage, finely
shredded

1 tablespoon (20 ml/¾ fl oz)
Japanese soy sauce

1 tablespoon (20 ml/¾ fl oz)
mirin (sweet cooking wine)

2 spring onions, thinly sliced

1 teaspoon sesame oil

Bring a large saucepan of salted water to the boil and gradually add the noodles, stirring to separate the strands. Cook for 2 minutes or until tender, drain well, then rinse under cold water to remove any excess starch. Drain noodles well again and divide between four large soup bowls.

Transfer a little of the dashi to a small bowl. Add the miso paste and blend until smooth. Meanwhile, allow tofu to come to room temperature. >

Heat the vegetable oil in a large heavy-based saucepan over medium heat. Add the carrot and stir-fry for a minute. Add the garlic and ginger, and stir-fry for another 30 seconds. Add the remaining dashi and bring to the boil, stir in the miso mixture until combined, return to the boil, then add the cabbage, soy and mirin, and cook for a further minute. Ladle mixture over the noodles, top with tofu and spring onions, drizzle with the sesame oil, and serve immediately.

- You can substitute other green vegetables for the cabbage: try snow peas, green beans or spinach leaves.
- Originating from China, ramen noodles are made from egg and wheat. They are available fresh, dried or 'instant' at Asian grocers.

Fried Noodles

Yakisoba

Serves 4

500 g (1 lb 2 oz) fresh
yakisoba noodles

120 g (4 oz) boneless pork
belly, cut into 2-cm (¾-in)
cubes

2 teaspoons finely grated fresh
ginger

2 cloves garlic, thinly sliced

1 teaspoon sesame oil

2 tablespoons (40 ml/1½ fl oz)
vegetable oil

100 g (3½ oz) fresh shiitake
mushrooms, stems discarded
and caps thinly sliced

4 spring onions, cut into
2.5-cm (1-in) lengths

1 carrot, thinly sliced

1 green capsicum, cut into
thin strips

½ Chinese cabbage, finely
shredded

3 tablespoons (60 ml/2 fl oz)
yakisoba sauce, to serve

nori flakes, to serve

2 tablespoons pickled ginger
(page 230), to serve

Place noodles in a large bowl, cover with boiling water and drain immediately. Loosen noodles to separate the strands.

In a bowl combine pork, ginger, garlic and sesame oil, stirring until well coated. Heat half the vegetable oil in a wok over medium–high heat. Add pork and stir-fry until browned and almost cooked (6–8 minutes), then remove from wok. Add mushrooms, spring onions, carrot and capsicum to wok, and stir-fry for 2 minutes. Add cabbage and stir-fry for another minute. >

Transfer contents of the wok to a large bowl and return wok to the heat. Heat remaining vegetable oil, add the drained noodles and stir-fry for a minute. Return the pork and vegetables to the wok, cover with a lid and steam for 1 minute. Remove the lid, add yakisoba sauce and stir quickly through the noodle mixture.

Divide the yakisoba noodles between four plates and serve sprinkled with nori flakes and pickled ginger.

Yakisoba noodles are wheat noodles similar to ramen: you can use hokkien noodles instead. Yakisoba sauce is available at Asian food stores.

Buckwheat Noodles

Soba

Serves 6 as a side dish

400 g (14 oz) dried soba noodles

DIPPING SAUCE

1½ cups (375 ml/11 fl oz) dashi stock I (page 34)

⅓ cup (80 ml/3 fl oz) Japanese soy sauce

⅓ cup (80 ml/3 fl oz) mirin (sweet cooking wine)

¼ teaspoon caster sugar

CONDIMENTS

2 spring onions, finely sliced

wasabi paste

½ sheet toasted nori, cut into fine shreds

a 3-cm (1¼-in) piece daikon, peeled and finely grated

Make the dipping sauce first. Combine dashi, soy, mirin and sugar in a small saucepan over medium heat and stir until sugar is dissolved. Transfer to a jug and refrigerate to chill.

Bring a large saucepan of lightly salted water to the boil. Add the noodles gradually so that they don't stick together. Bring water back to the boil, then add a cup of cold water and allow to come back to the boil. Add another cup of cold water, return to the boil again and simmer until the noodles are just cooked. Remove from heat, drain noodles, rinse under cold water and drain well again. Refrigerate until chilled.

To serve, mound the noodles on four plates with condiments and dipping sauce placed in individual dishes for each person. Guests add condiments to the dipping sauce, to taste, and then use chopsticks to dip the noodles into the seasoned sauce.

Udon Noodles with Chicken & Spring Onions in Broth

Serves 6

400 g (14 oz) dried udon noodles

450 g (14 oz) skinless chicken breast fillets, cut crossways into 5-mm (¼-in) slices

8 spring onions, finely sliced

shichimi togarashi (seven-spice mix), to serve (optional)

BROTH

1.5 L (3 pt 3 fl oz) dashi stock I (page 34)

2 tablespoons (40 ml/1½ fl oz) Japanese soy sauce

2 tablespoons (40 ml/1½ fl oz) dark soy sauce

2 tablespoons (40 ml/1½ fl oz) mirin (sweet cooking wine)

2 teaspoons caster sugar

Bring a large saucepan of salted water to the boil. Add the noodles, bring water back to the boil and cook for 15–20 minutes (or according to packet instructions), until just cooked. Turn off heat and allow noodles to stand for 5 minutes. Drain noodles, rinse under cold water to stop the cooking process, then drain well again and set aside.

Meanwhile prepare the broth by combining the dashi, soy sauces, mirin and sugar in a saucepan over medium–high heat. Add the chicken slices to the broth and simmer for about 5 minutes, until just cooked. Now add the spring onions (reserve 1 tablespoonful for garnish) and noodles, and heat through. >

Transfer noodles to serving bowls, then pour the broth over. Garnish each bowl with a scattering of spring onion, and pass around the shichimi (if using) for sprinkling.

If fresh udon noodles are available, use 750 g (1 lb 10 oz) and cook in boiling salted water for 5 minutes, or until soft.

Stir-fried Harusame Noodles with Greens & Shiitakes

Serves 4–6 as light meal

400 g (14 oz) harusame noodles (see note page 170)

2 teaspoons vegetable oil

1 teaspoon grated fresh ginger

6 fresh shiitake mushrooms, stems discarded and caps thinly sliced

2 tablespoons (40 ml/1½ fl oz) Japanese soy sauce

1 tablespoon (20 ml/¾ fl oz) mirin (sweet cooking wine)

2 cups loosely packed mizuna (or baby spinach) leaves

½ sheet toasted nori, cut into fine shreds, for garnish

1 spring onion, finely chopped

1 tablespoon sesame seeds, toasted (optional)

Soak the noodles in a large bowl of hot water for 10 minutes until tender. Drain well. Cut into 10–15 cm (4–6 in) lengths.

Heat oil in a non-stick frying pan over medium heat. Add the ginger and mushrooms and stir-fry for 2 minutes until mushrooms are softened. Add the drained noodles, the soy and mirin, and using chopsticks toss gently to combine and coat noodles in sauce. Cook for 2 minutes until warmed through. Add the mizuna leaves and quickly toss through. Remove from the heat.

Serve immediately, garnished with a scattering of nori shreds and spring onions. Sprinkle with sesame seeds, if using.

Red Rice

Sekihan

Serves 6–8 as a side dish

½ cup dried adzuki beans,
  rinsed

3 cups glutinous rice
  (see note page 222)

½ teaspoon salt

2 tablespoons black sesame
  seeds, toasted

Place adzuki beans and 3 cups (750 ml/25 fl oz) cold water in a medium-sized saucepan over high heat and bring to the boil. Reduce to a simmer and cook for 15–20 minutes or until outer layer of the beans is just beginning to soften. Drain beans, reserving the cooking water.

Put the rice in a large bowl and rinse under cold water, swirling the rice around, until water runs clear. Drain well.

Combine 1½ cups (375 ml/12½ fl oz) of the reserved bean liquid with an equal quantity of water. Place the rice, salt and measured liquid in a medium-sized saucepan, and set aside for 3 hours.

Place the drained beans on top of the rice, cover saucepan with a lid and set over a high heat. Bring to the boil, reduce heat, and simmer gently for 15 minutes until all the liquid is absorbed. Remove pan from heat and set aside for 10 minutes, keeping the lid on.

Stir the rice to mix the beans through. Spoon mixture onto a platter or serving dish, and sprinkle with the sesame seeds. Serve warm or at room temperature.

- Red rice is traditionally served at celebrations such as weddings, or for holidays. It would be served as one of a selection of dishes.

- Adzuki are small red beans often used in sweet dishes: they're available at Asian food stores and many supermarkets.

- This dish can also be cooked in a rice cooker (follow the manufacturer's instructions).

Rice Balls

Onigiri

Serves 6

1 × 100-g (3½-oz) can tuna
in brine, drained

1½ tablespoons Japanese
mayonnaise

a few drops Japanese soy
sauce

double quantity freshly cooked
basic steamed rice (page 233)

1 sheet toasted nori, cut into
6 strips

sea salt

sansho pepper

Place tuna and mayonnaise in a bowl and mix well. Add a few drops of soy,
to taste.

Take about ¼ cup of the still-warm rice in your left hand and form a hollow in the centre. Place about two teaspoons of tuna mixture inside and
enclose by shaping the rice into a ball. Wrap a strip of nori around the ball.
Repeat with the remaining rice and tuna filling, to make another five balls.

Place rice balls on a serving plate and sprinkle with sea salt and sansho
pepper just before serving.

❀ Onigiri are a popular item in bento boxes. They can be made with
all kinds of fillings and are a great way to use up leftovers, such
as: chicken marinated and deep-fried (page 171), simmered shiitake
mushrooms (page 65), simmered pumpkin (page 61), fried pork cutlet
(page 157).

Chicken & Rice

Tori-gohan

Serves 2 as a main or 4 as a starter

- 1⅓ cups Japanese short-grain rice
- 1 skinless chicken breast fillet, cut crossways into strips 3 mm (⅛ in) wide
- 4 dried shiitake mushrooms
- 1 L (34 fl oz) dashi stock II (page 35)
- 1 tablespoon (20 ml/¾ fl oz) mirin (sweet cooking wine)
- ½ teaspoon salt
- 1 teaspoon Japanese soy sauce
- ⅓ cup shelled fresh peas
- 1 tablespoon chopped flat-leaf parsley or shiso (beefsteak plant) leaves, for garnish

MARINADE

- ⅓ cup (80 ml/3 fl oz) Japanese soy sauce
- 1 tablespoon (20 ml/¾ fl oz) sake (Japanese rice wine)
- 1 tablespoon (15 g/½ oz) caster sugar

Rinse the rice under cold running water until water runs clear. Place rice in a bowl, cover with water and leave to soak for 1 hour.

Now prepare the marinade by placing all the ingredients in a bowl and stirring until the sugar dissolves. Add the chicken strips and toss to coat well, then cover and refrigerate for 30 minutes.

Soak the mushrooms in a bowl of hot water for 30 minutes. Drain, then cut off and discard the stems and slice the caps thinly. Set aside. >

Drain the rice and transfer to a medium-sized saucepan. Stir in the dashi, mirin, salt and soy until combined. Add the sliced mushrooms, peas and the drained chicken pieces, discarding any excess marinade. Place the saucepan over medium–high heat, bring to the boil, stir to combine and boil for 2 minutes. Cover tightly with a lid, reduce heat to low and cook for a further 7 minutes, without lifting the lid. Remove pan (lid still on) from the heat and set aside for 5 minutes.

Ladle mixture into bowls and sprinkle with chopped parsley or shiso before serving.

Green Tea Rice

Ochazuke

Serves 4

3 cups freshly cooked basic
   steamed rice (page 233)

2 cups (500 ml/17 fl oz) hot
   brewed green tea

½ cup chopped mitsuba
   (Japanese parsley) (optional)

Japanese pickles (optional)

nori flakes, for garnish

1 tablespoon white sesame
   seeds, toasted

wasabi paste, to serve

Spoon the hot rice into four individual bowls. Pour the hot tea over, and scatter with the mitsuba leaves or pickles, as desired. Top with a sprinkling of nori flakes and sesame seeds, and serve immediately, accompanied by a small dish of wasabi.

- For a version with salmon (sake no ochazuke), replace the steamed rice with 1 quantity salmon cooked on rice (page 110).
- Use homemade pickles such as the pickled cabbage and celery (page 229), or bought pickles like daikon or eggplant.

Prawn Sukiyaki on Rice

Sukiyaki donburi

Serves 4 as a light meal

200 g (7 oz) shirataki noodles

1 tablespoon (20 ml/¾ fl oz) vegetable oil

2 teaspoons sesame oil

12 raw (green) prawns, shelled and deveined but tails left intact

2 spring onions, cut diagonally into 2-cm (¾-in) lengths

200 g (7 oz) enoki mushrooms, ends trimmed

3 tablespoons (60 ml/2 fl oz) mirin (sweet cooking wine)

1 tablespoon (20 ml/¾ fl oz) sake (Japanese rice wine)

3 tablespoons (60 ml/2 fl oz) combination soy sauce (page 236), plus extra if needed

2 cups mizuna or rocket leaves

double quantity freshly cooked basic steamed rice (page 233)

pickled ginger (page 230), to serve

Soak the noodles in a bowl of hot water for 5 minutes. Drain well, then cut into 10-cm (4-in) lengths and set aside.

Heat both oils in a heavy-based non-stick frying pan over high heat. Add the prawns and spring onions, and stir-fry for 1–2 minutes, until prawns are starting to turn opaque and are light-golden in places. Reduce heat to medium, add the mushrooms and stir-fry for 30 seconds. Add the mirin, sake and combination soy sauce, and simmer for 2 minutes. >

Stir in the drained noodles and the mizuna until combined, then cook for a minute or until all ingredients are warmed through and the prawns are cooked.

Spoon prepared rice into bowls and top with the prawn mixture. Serve immediately, with pickled ginger and extra combination soy sauce, if desired.

❋ Shirataki are thin, gelatinous noodles with a bland flavour. They are available at Asian food stores.

Fried Pork with Egg on Rice

Katsudon

Serves 4

1 quantity fried pork cutlets (page 157)

2 teaspoons vegetable oil

1 small onion, finely chopped

1½ cups (375 ml/12 fl oz) dashi stock II (page 35)

⅓ cup (80 ml/4 fl oz) Japanese soy sauce

3 tablespoons (60 ml/2 fl oz) mirin (sweet cooking wine)

a small bunch (100 g/3½ oz) mitsuba (Japanese parsley), coarsely chopped

6 eggs, lightly beaten

double quantity freshly cooked basic steamed rice (page 233)

Cut the pork into slices 2.5 cm (1 in) thick.

Heat the oil in a non-stick frying pan over medium heat. Add the onion and cook for 5 minutes until softened. Add the dashi, soy and mirin, and bring to the boil. Reduce heat to a simmer, add the mitsuba, then pour in the beaten eggs and stir gently to mix through. Cover with a lid and cook for 1 minute, or until the egg is just set.

Take care not to overcook the rice, as it should still be moist. Divide rice between four deep bowls and top with sliced pork. Spoon one-quarter of the egg mixture over each portion, and serve immediately.

Salmon Cooked on Rice

Serves 4

1½ cups Japanese short-grain rice

400 g (14 oz) salmon fillet, bones removed

1 teaspoon sea salt

1½ cups (375 ml/12½ fl oz) dashi stock II (page 35)

1½ tablespoons (30 ml/1 fl oz) Japanese soy sauce

1 tablespoon (20 ml/¾ fl oz) mirin (sweet cooking wine)

CONDIMENTS

a 3-cm (1¼-in) piece fresh ginger, finely grated

nori flakes

Japanese soy sauce

Rinse the rice under cold water until water runs clear. Drain, and set aside in the strainer for 30 minutes.

Preheat griller to high.

Rub salmon skin with the salt and place salmon, skin side up, under the griller for 1–2 minutes until skin turns a light golden brown.

Transfer drained rice to a medium-sized saucepan, add the dashi, soy and mirin, and stir to combine. Place the salmon on top of the rice, set saucepan over medium–high heat and bring to the boil. Cover tightly with lid, reduce heat to low and cook for 10 minutes without lifting the lid. Remove pan (lid still on) from the heat and set aside for 5 minutes. >

When ready to serve, gently stir the fish into the rice, flaking the flesh to distribute evenly. Take the pan to the table and spoon into individual bowls. Place the condiments in small serving dishes so that each person can season their own portion as desired.

Rice Omelette

Serves 2 as a main or 4 as a side dish

1½ tablespoons (30 ml/1 fl oz) vegetable oil

2 spring onions, finely chopped

1 clove garlic, crushed

1 teaspoon finely chopped fresh ginger

100 g (3½ oz) chicken or pork mince

2 fresh shiitake mushrooms, stems discarded and caps diced

¼ cup chopped broccoli florets

3 tablespoons (60 ml/2 fl oz) tomato sauce

1 quantity basic steamed rice (page 233)

4 eggs

1 teaspoon Japanese soy sauce

tonkatsu sauce (page 157), to serve

Heat 1 tablespoon of the oil in a non-stick frying pan over medium heat. Add spring onions, garlic and ginger, and cook for 1 minute or until aromatic. Add the chicken or pork mince and stir-fry for 6–8 minutes until meat is cooked. Add mushrooms and broccoli, and stir-fry for another minute. Stir in the tomato sauce and rice until well combined, remove from heat, cover pan, and set aside.

Lightly beat the eggs with the soy sauce. Heat the remaining oil over medium heat in a non-stick frying pan about 20 cm (8 in) in diameter, or in a Japanese omelette pan. >

Pour in half the egg mixture, tilt pan to allow the mixture to spread evenly over base of pan, then cook for 1 minute or until eggs have almost set. Spoon half of the rice mixture along the centre of the omelette. Using a spatula, gently fold the sides of the omelette over to cover the rice. Place a plate over the pan and turn pan upside down to invert omelette onto the plate. Repeat process with the remaining egg and rice mixtures.

Serve with tonkatsu sauce or extra tomato sauce, if desired.

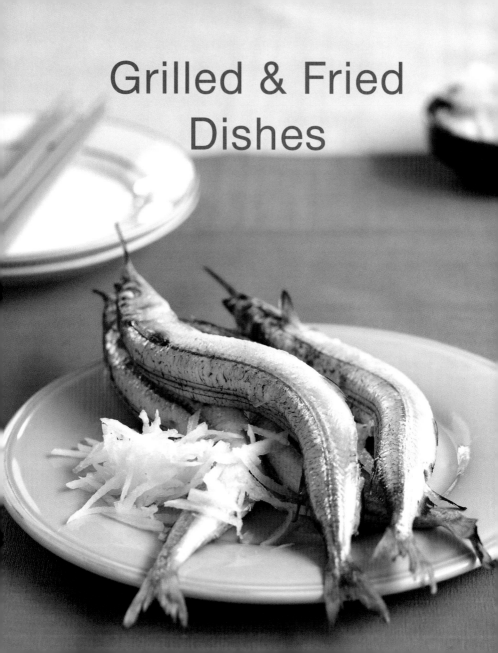

Grilled & Fried Dishes

In Japan, the technique of cooking food directly over a grill (usually charcoal) is known as yakimono. The high heat achieves a crisp, flavourful surface and moist, tender inside. Skewers are often used: when grilling fish, twist the skewers several times during cooking to prevent the flesh sticking when you remove the skewers. In tataki dishes (see page 165) the meat is seared, keeping the centre rare, and then served sashimi-style.

Deep-frying (agemono) was introduced to Japan via the Chinese and southern Europeans, though in true Japanese style the method has been refined to simple, subtle perfection. The food may be coated in panko (Japanese breadcrumbs), flour, or a light batter. The oil for deep-frying should have a mild flavour (such as vegetable or sunflower oil). Shallow-frying uses a small amount of oil and includes pan-frying and stir-frying.

‹ Garfish on Skewers (page 118)

Garfish on Skewers

Sayori no-shio-yaki

Serves 4 as a starter

4 whole garfish or whiting
(20 cm/8 in long), cleaned

3 tablespoons (60 ml/2 fl oz)
mirin (sweet cooking wine)

2 tablespoons sea salt

¼ daikon, peeled and finely
grated

1 teaspoon ginger juice
(see note page 47), to serve
(optional)

Soak four bamboo skewers in water for 30 minutes.

Thread each fish onto a skewer, so it forms an undulating 'S' shape. Place fish on a plate and drizzle with the mirin (both outside and inside the cavity) then sprinkle the surfaces with the salt.

Preheat griller to high.

Place skewered fish on a lightly oiled wire rack under the griller (about 8 cm/3 in from the heat) and cook for 10–12 minutes or until flesh becomes opaque. (Occasionally give the skewers a twist, as this will help them slip out easily when fish is cooked.)

Remove fish from heat and pull out the skewers. Serve immediately with grated daikon, and ginger juice if desired.

Steam-grilled Chicken

Tori mushiyaki

Serves 4

6 chicken thigh fillets, skin on

8 fresh shiitake mushrooms,
stems discarded

1 tablespoon (20 ml/¾ fl oz)
sake (Japanese rice wine)

2 tablespoons (40 ml/1½ fl oz)
Japanese soy sauce

2 tablespoons (40 ml/1½ fl oz)
freshly squeezed lemon juice

1 teaspoon salt

Cut the chicken into 2.5-cm (1-in) chunks. Add to a bowl with the mushrooms, sprinkle with the sake and set aside for 5 minutes.

Meanwhile, make a dipping sauce by combining the soy and lemon juice, and divide between four small bowls. Set aside until needed.

Have ready four sheets of aluminium foil, each 30 cm (12 in) square. Place a quarter of the chicken and mushroom mixture in the centre of each piece of foil. Sprinkle a little salt over each. Fold foil over to form a package, sealing all the edges well to prevent juices escaping during cooking.

Preheat barbecue grill to high. Place the foil parcels directly on the grill and cook for 4 minutes, then turn over and cook the other side for 3 minutes. Transfer the packages to serving plates.

To serve, carefully split the packages open to reveal the contents, and accompany with the bowls of dipping sauce.

Chicken Kebabs

Yakitori

Serves 6

1 kg (2 lb 3 oz) skinless chicken thigh fillets, cut into 2.5-cm (1-in) cubes

12 spring onions (white parts only), cut into 2.5-cm (1-in) lengths

shichimi togarashi (seven-spice mix), for garnish (optional)

YAKITORI SAUCE

3 tablespoons (60 ml/2 fl oz) sake (Japanese rice wine)

½ cup (125 ml/4 fl oz) Japanese soy sauce

½ cup (125 ml/4 fl oz) mirin (sweet cooking wine)

1 tablespoon (15 g/1 oz) caster sugar

Soak 12 bamboo skewers in water for 30 minutes.

To make the yakitori sauce, place the sake, soy, mirin and sugar in a small saucepan over medium heat. Bring to a simmer and cook for 3 minutes or until the sauce glazes the back of a spoon (thin syrupy consistency). Set aside to cool until ready to use.

Preheat griller to medium–high.

Thread three pieces of chicken onto a skewer, alternating with spring-onion lengths. Repeat with remaining skewers, chicken and spring onions. >

Brush the chicken skewers with the yakitori sauce and place under the griller on a foil-lined baking tray. Cook, turning often, for 3 minutes. Remove, brush skewers all over with more sauce, return to the grill and cook for a further 1–2 minutes until chicken is cooked and golden-glazed.

Serve immediately, accompanied with the spice mix for sprinkling.

❀ Instead of chicken thighs, you can use chicken livers or chicken wings, or a selection of all three.

Crispy Sesame & Ginger Chicken

Serves 4

8 chicken thigh fillets, skin on

MARINADE

1 tablespoon (20 ml/¾ fl oz) sake (Japanese rice wine)

1 tablespoon (20 ml/¾ fl oz) Japanese soy sauce

1 tablespoon (20 ml/¾ fl oz) sesame oil

a 2.5-cm (1-in) piece fresh ginger, finely grated

Use a sharp knife to make shallow, diagonal cuts across the skin of each thigh fillet.

Mix the sake, soy, oil and ginger in a ceramic or glass bowl, add the chicken and turn to coat evenly on all sides. Cover, and refrigerate for 1 hour.

Preheat oven to 200°C (390°F). Place the chicken thighs, skin side up, on a baking tray lined with foil. Bake for 25 minutes, or until chicken is cooked through and skin is golden and crisp.

Slice the chicken into wide strips, and serve with rice and salad.

❀ Instead of cooking the chicken in the oven, thread two bamboo skewers (first soaked in water for 30 minutes) through each thigh fillet. Cook chicken under a preheated griller or on a barbecue for 8 minutes on each side (skin side first) or until cooked through.

Mixed Grill

Teppanyaki

Serves 4

600 g (1 lb 5 oz) beef eye fillet, trimmed of sinew and fat

2½ tablespoons (50 ml/1¾ fl oz) vegetable oil

salt and ground white pepper

4 lemon or lime wedges

a 3-cm (1¼-in) piece daikon, peeled and finely grated, and excess moisture squeezed out

ponzu sauce (page 237) or Japanese soy sauce, for dipping

2 capsicums, cut lengthways into 8 pieces

4 fresh shiitake mushrooms, stems discarded

1½ cups bean sprouts

You will need a portable electric or gas hotplate for this dish, as it is cooked at the table.

Cut the beef into four slices. Brush all over with 1 tablespoon (20 ml/¾ fl oz) of the oil and rub in, then season with salt and pepper.

Place portable hotplate in the centre of the dining table. Have four serving plates with lemon wedges, daikon and individual bowls of dipping sauce ready for each person. ➤

Heat a flat cast-iron grill plate or heavy-based frying pan over high heat. Cook beef for 3 minutes on each side (for rare) or to your liking. Remove meat and rest it for 5 minutes.

Meanwhile, heat remaining oil on grill plate or in frying pan. Stir-fry the capsicum and mushrooms for 3–5 minutes until cooked through, and transfer to a serving plate. Then stir-fry the bean sprouts for a minute, and add to serving plate. Cut the meat into 1-cm (⅜-in) slices, and serve.

Each person can squeeze lemon or lime juice over their portion and then dip it into the dipping sauce.

❀ You can use a wide selection of other vegetables and meats for this dish – try sliced onion, tomato, zucchini, eggplant, chicken or prawns.

Grilled Eel

Unagi kabayaki

Serves 4

2 eels, filleted but with skin on (ask your fishmonger to do this)

3 tablespoons (60 ml/2 fl oz) Japanese soy sauce

3 tablespoons (60 ml/2 fl oz) sake (Japanese rice wine)

2 tablespoons (30 g/1 oz) caster sugar

sesame oil, for brushing

sansho pepper

double quantity basic steamed rice (page 233), to serve

Cut the eel fillets into 10-cm (4-in) lengths.

Using a saucepan with a steamer section, half-fill the pan with water and bring to the boil over high heat. Line the steamer with baking paper. Steam the eel in batches for 15 minutes, each time arranging the pieces on the baking paper in one layer. Remove and set aside.

Combine the soy, sake and caster sugar in a small bowl. Preheat griller to medium–high.

Line a baking tray with aluminium foil and brush lightly with sesame oil. Place the eel fillets on the tray, and brush generously on all sides with the soy mixture. Grill for 8–10 minutes, turning frequently and brushing with the marinade each time you turn the pieces, until glazed and golden-brown.

Sprinkle eel with sansho pepper and serve immediately with steamed rice.

Skewered Prawns

Serves 4 as a starter

**12 large raw (green) king
 prawns**

2 teaspoons sake

1 tablespoon sea salt

Japanese soy sauce, to serve

4 lemon wedges, to serve

Insert a metal skewer lengthways through the centre of each prawn. Place prawns on a tray and sprinkle with the sake (it acts as a tenderiser). Leave for 5 minutes.

Preheat grill pan or barbecue grill to high.

Sprinkle the prawns on all sides with the salt. Place on the grill and cook for 2–3 minutes, then turn over and grill the other side for 2 minutes or until opaque and just cooked through.

Remove prawns from skewers and serve immediately with soy sauce for dipping, and the lemon wedges alongside. Provide a bowl of hot water containing lemon slices, for cleaning fingers, and an empty bowl for discarded prawn shells.

Tofu on a Stick

Tofu dengaku

Serves 6 as a starter

100 g (3½ oz) white miso paste

1 egg yolk

1 tablespoon (20 ml/¾ fl oz) sake (Japanese rice wine)

1 tablespoon (20 ml/¾ fl oz) mirin (sweet cooking wine)

1 tablespoon (15 g/½ oz) caster sugar

2 tablespoons (40 ml/1½ fl oz) dashi stock II (page 35)

½ teaspoon ginger juice (see note page 47)

500 g (1 lb 2 oz) firm tofu

sesame oil, for brushing

nori flakes or black sesame seeds, for garnish

You will need six two-pronged bamboo forks (available at Asian food stores) or 12 bamboo skewers. Soak in water for 30 minutes.

Place the miso, egg yolk, sake, mirin and sugar in a heatproof bowl and set over a saucepan of simmering water (make sure the water is not touching the base of the bowl) and whisk until smooth. Gradually add the dashi and continue whisking until stock is incorporated and the mixture has thickened (about 1 minute). Remove bowl from the heat, then stir in the ginger juice and set aside until needed.

Preheat griller to high.

Meanwhile, cut the tofu into six rectangles 2 cm × 5 cm (¾ in × 2 in) and about 1.5 cm (⅝ in) thick. Brush lightly with oil and place on a foil-lined baking tray. Insert a bamboo fork or two bamboo skewers into the narrow side of each tofu slice. Place baking tray under grill and cook tofu for 2–3 minutes on each side (turn very carefully) or until it turns a speckled golden brown.

Working quickly, spread the miso mixture evenly on the upper surface of each tofu piece. Replace under the grill for about a minute or until miso is bubbling and heated through. Sprinkle with nori or black sesame seeds before serving.

Serve immediately.

❀ You can use red miso for the topping, instead of white.

Scallops Grilled in Soy Sauce

Serves 4 as a starter or snack

12 scallops on the shell

2 tablespoons (40 ml/1½ fl oz)
  sake

2 tablespoons (40 ml/1½ fl oz)
  Japanese soy sauce

parsley sprigs, for garnish

1 lemon, cut into wedges

Preheat griller or barbecue grill to high.

Remove scallops from the shells, then clean and rinse scallops and shells under cold water, and pat dry with paper towel. Replace scallops on the shells. Drizzle the sake and soy evenly over each scallop, then grill for 2–3 minutes or until the scallops become opaque and are just cooked through.

Serve immediately, garnished with parsley sprigs and with lemon wedges for squeezing.

Salt-grilled Whole Trout

Ayu no shioyaki

Serves 4

4 × 250-g (9-oz) small whole
  trout, cleaned

2 tablespoons sea salt

basic steamed rice (page 233),
  to serve

lemon wedges, to serve

pickled ginger (page 230),
  to serve

Japanese soy sauce, to serve

Soak eight bamboo skewers in water for 30 minutes.

To skewer whole fish in the traditional manner of 'wave skewering', place the fish with the head facing to your right. Insert a skewer behind the eye, push it lengthways through the body (taking care not to pierce the other side) and then out the other side about 4 cm (1½ in) away. Bend the fish slightly and insert the tip of the skewer again, beyond the belly, then back out again on the top at the base of the tail. Repeat this process with a second skewer, running parallel about 2 cm (¾ in) from the first.

Turn skewered fish over, so the heads are facing left. Cut a shallow slash across the centre of each fish. Using your fingers, rub the tails and fins generously with salt (which will form a crust when cooked, and is for decorative appearance only). Lightly rub more salt over both sides of fish, to season.

Preheat griller or charcoal grill to high. If using a charcoal grill, lightly oil the rack and place the fish slashed side down. If cooking under a grill, place fish slashed side up on an oiled wire rack sitting on a baking tray. Cook fish for 5 minutes or until the skin begins to bubble up and pink beading forms on the flesh. Carefully turn fish over and grill the other side for 4–5 minutes or until the flesh becomes opaque.

Remove skewers and serve the fish (head facing left) with steamed rice, accompanied with lemon wedges and pickled ginger. Pass soy sauce around for dipping.

✿ Alternatively use fish fillets such as mullet or red mullet (the overall cooking time will be shorter). Cook fillets skin side first.

Salmon Grilled with Soy & Sake

Yuan-yaki

Serves 4 as a starter or small dish

225 g (8 oz) salmon fillet
taken from belly area

2 tablespoons (40 ml/1½ fl oz)
Japanese soy sauce

2 tablespoons (40 ml/1½ fl oz)
mirin (sweet cooking wine)

2 tablespoons (40 ml/1½ fl oz)
sake (Japanese rice wine)

2 teaspoons freshly squeezed
lemon juice

a 2-cm (¾-in) piece fresh
ginger, thinly sliced

lemon wedges, for garnish

Soak four bamboo skewers in water for 30 minutes.

Cut the salmon into four even-sized lengths. Combine the soy, mirin, sake, lemon juice and ginger in a shallow dish. Add the salmon, turn to coat in marinade, then cover and refrigerate for 2 hours, turning occasionally.

Preheat a grill pan or barbecue grill to medium–high. Drain excess marinade from salmon and insert a skewer along the length of each piece. Grill salmon, skin side down, for 2 minutes or until skin is crisp and starts to bubble. Turn carefully and cook the other side for about 2 minutes, twisting skewers occasionally to loosen.

Remove skewers and transfer salmon pieces to serving plate. Garnish with lemon wedges.

Crispy Deep-fried Prawns

Kesyo-age

Serves 4 as a starter

- 12 raw (green) king prawns, shelled and deveined but tail left intact
- 1 sheet toasted nori, cut into 12 strips
- 1 quantity tempura batter (page 239)
- 1½ cups (150 g/5 oz) coarse rice flour

- vegetable or sunflower oil for deep-frying
- lemon wedges and sea salt, to serve
- tempura dipping sauce (page 160), to serve (optional)

Cut three shallow incisions across the underside (belly) of each prawn to prevent them curling during cooking. Wrap a strip of nori around each prawn tail.

Prepare the batter just before using, as this helps keep it light. Place batter in a bowl and spread the rice flour on a plate. Pour oil into deep-fryer or wok, to a minimum depth of 5 cm (2 in). Heat to 180°C (360°F): the oil is ready when you add a drop of batter and it rises instantly and is surrounded by tiny bubbles.

Holding one prawn by the tail, dip into the tempura batter (be careful not to coat the nori strip or the tail). Working quickly, then dip the prawn into the rice flour to coat evenly and slide the prawn into the hot oil.

Deep-fry for 2–3 minutes or until light golden all over. Remove prawn from oil and drain on paper towel. Repeat process with the remaining prawns.

Serve with lemon wedges and salt, or tempura dipping sauce.

- You can keep cooked prawns warm in a 120°C (250°F) oven for about 5 minutes as you cook the remainder.
- Coarse rice flour (domyoji) is less finely ground than the regular variety, and gives the coating an extra-crunchy texture.

Beef & Vegetable Rolls

Makes about 32

600 g (1 lb 5 oz) beef sirloin
steak, trimmed

8 thin asparagus spears,
ends trimmed

4 fresh shiitake mushrooms
(or 3 simmered shiitake
mushrooms – page 65)

8 spring onions

MARINADE

⅓ cup (80 ml/3 fl oz) soy sauce

2 tablespoons (40 ml/1½ fl oz)
sake

⅓ cup (80 ml/3 fl oz) mirin
(sweet cooking wine)

Ask the butcher to slice the steak into 32 paper-thin slices for you. Alternatively, freeze the meat for 2 hours (which makes it easier to slice very thinly) and slice as per instructions on following page.

Soak 16 bamboo skewers in water for 30 minutes.

Cut the asparagus into 7-cm (2½-in) lengths and cook in a saucepan of boiling salted water for 1 minute, or until just tender. Drain, plunge into a bowl of cold water to stop the cooking process, then drain well and pat dry with paper towel. Cut mushroom caps into 5-mm (¼-in) slices. Cut white parts of the spring onions into 7-cm (2½-in) lengths and halve lengthways. >

If preparing the beef yourself, use a carving knife to cut about 32 paper-thin slices along the length of the meat, each measuring 5 cm × 10 cm (2 in × 4 in). Place two strips lengthways, slightly overlapping, to form a thin 'sheet'. Gently press the overlapping edges to seal.

Lay one beef sheet on a work surface. Arrange a length of spring onion and asparagus, and two pieces of mushroom, along the edge closest to you and carefully roll up the meat to enclose. Tie the roll securely with string. Repeat with remaining meat pieces and vegetables, to make another 15 rolls.

Combine all marinade ingredients in a shallow ceramic dish. Add the rolls and turn to coat evenly. Cover, and refrigerate for an hour, turning occasionally.

Preheat the griller to medium–high. Drain the beef rolls, reserving any excess marinade for basting. Place two rolls side by side and push two skewers, 3 cm (1¼ in) apart, crossways through them and running parallel, to keep the rolls flat. Repeat with the remaining rolls and skewers. Grill the rolls for about 3 minutes on each side, until browned and cooked through, basting a couple of times.

Remove the skewers and string, cut rolls in half crossways, and serve immediately – as a snack with drinks or as a main served with rice and a salad.

❀ Pre-sliced steak is available frozen at many Asian food stores.

Grilled Lobster

Onigara-yaki

Serves 2

1 large lobster tail

1½ teaspoons sake (Japanese rice wine)

2 teaspoons Japanese soy sauce

2 tablespoons (40 ml/1½ fl oz) mirin (sweet cooking wine)

1 egg yolk

4 lemon wedges, to serve

sansho pepper

Preheat griller to high. Cut lobster tail in half lengthways and place on a baking tray lined with aluminium foil.

In a small bowl combine the sake, soy, mirin and egg yolk, and brush generously over the cut side of the lobster. Place tray with lobster tail under the grill (about 10 cm/4 in from the heat). Cook for 12–15 minutes or until lobster flesh turns opaque.

Serve immediately, with lemon wedges alongside and sansho pepper for sprinkling.

🌸 You can replace the lobster tail with 6 large raw (green) prawns, shelled and deveined but tails intact. Insert a metal skewer lengthways through the centre of each prawn, brush with the sauce and grill for 5 minutes or until flesh turns opaque. Withdraw the skewers before serving as above.

Japanese Pancakes

Okonomiyaki

Serves 4

1 cup finely shredded Chinese
cabbage

¼ teaspoon salt

2 cups (300 g/10½ oz) plain
flour

¾ cup (185 ml/6 fl oz) dashi
stock II (page 35) or water

3 eggs

3 spring onions, finely sliced

1 small red capsicum, diced

6 raw (green) prawns, shelled
and deveined

100 g (3¼ oz) octopus
tentacles or squid, thinly
sliced

vegetable oil for frying

OKONOMIYAKI SAUCE

1 teaspoon cornflour

3 tablespoons (60 ml/2 fl oz)
tomato sauce

2 tablespoons (40 ml/1½ fl oz)
Worcestershire sauce

2 tablespoons (40 ml/1½ fl oz)
Japanese soy sauce

2 teaspoons ginger juice (see
note page 47)

1 tablespoon (15 g/½ oz) caster
sugar

CONDIMENTS

Japanese mayonnaise

nori flakes

dried bonito flakes

pickled ginger (page 230)

You will need a frying pan about 20–25 cm (8–9 in) in diameter.

Toss the cabbage with the salt, then set aside for 10 minutes. Squeeze out
any excess moisture and pat dry with paper towel.

Place flour in a bowl and make a well in the centre. Pour in dashi and eggs, then whisk in the flour until batter is smooth. Set aside for 20 minutes.

Meanwhile, prepare the sauce. Mix the cornflour into a tablespoon of water until smooth, then set aside. Place all the remaining ingredients in a small saucepan over medium–high heat and bring to the boil. Reduce heat to low, stir in the cornflour mixture and then cook for 3–5 minutes or until sauce thickens. Set aside.

Stir the cabbage, spring onions, capsicum, prawns and octopus or squid into the batter, and combine well. Heat 2 teaspoons of oil in a frying pan over medium–high heat. Spoon in a quarter of the batter and allow to spread over base of pan. Cook for 5–7 minutes, until golden underneath, then turn over and cook the other side for 3–5 minutes or until cooked through and golden. Repeat process with the remaining batter to make three more pancakes.

To serve, spread some okonomiyaki sauce and then some mayonnaise over each pancake, and let people help themselves to the other condiments as desired. Eat immediately.

Prepared okonomiyaki sauce is available at Asian food stores. The seafood can be replaced with meat such as thinly sliced or minced chicken, pork or beef. For a vegetarian option, use sliced mushrooms, spinach, diced firm tofu, or any diced vegetables.

Pork Potsticker Dumplings

Gyoza

Makes 24

1½ cups finely shredded
  Chinese cabbage

¼ teaspoon salt

250 g (9 oz) pork mince

½ cup finely chopped spring
  onions

2 cloves garlic, crushed

1 teaspoon finely grated fresh
  ginger (collect the juice)

1 tablespoon (20 ml/¾ fl oz)
  sake (Japanese rice wine)

1 tablespoon (20 ml/¾ fl oz)
  Japanese soy sauce

1 tablespoon (20 ml/¾ fl oz)
  mirin (sweet cooking wine)

24 gyoza wrappers

potato starch or cornflour,
  for dusting

2 teaspoons sesame oil

2 tablespoons (40 ml/1½ fl oz)
  vegetable oil

DIPPING SAUCE

3 tablespoons (60 ml/2 fl oz)
  Japanese soy sauce

3 tablespoons (60 ml/2 fl oz)
  Japanese rice vinegar

1 teaspoon sesame oil,
  or to taste

Place cabbage in a bowl, sprinkle with salt, toss to mix through and then set aside for 20 minutes. Squeeze to extract any excess moisture.

To prepare the dipping sauce, combine the soy and vinegar and then add sesame oil to taste.

Put pork, cabbage, spring onions, garlic, ginger (and juice), sake, soy and mirin in a medium-sized bowl and mix well. >

Place a gyoza wrapper on a clean work surface and place a heaped tea-spoonful of the pork filling in the centre. Wet the edges of the pastry with water, then press together to enclose filling and form a crescent. Using fingertips, make folds or pleats along the sealed edge. (Or omit this step and leave the dumpling as a simple semicircle shape.) Place dumpling, seam side up, on a tray lined with cling wrap and dusted with potato starch. Repeat process with the remaining filling and wrappers. Very lightly dust the tops of the dumplings with more potato starch.

Heat half the sesame oil and half the vegetable oil in a large heavy-based non-stick frying pan over medium–high heat. Shake dumplings to remove excess flour, then fry half of them, flat side down, for 2 minutes or until the bases are golden and crisp. Pour in ⅔ cup (150 ml/5 fl oz) cold water, place lid on pan, reduce heat to low–medium and cook dumplings for a further 8–10 minutes. Remove the lid, increase heat to medium and cook until all the water has evaporated and the bases of the dumplings start to crisp. Transfer to a serving plate. Repeat with remaining oil and gyoza.

Serve gyoza hot, with the dipping sauce in small bowls.

❀ Gyoza wrappers are available (usually in 200-g/7-oz packets) at Asian food stores. Traditionally, garlic chives (nira) are used instead of the spring onions and garlic: if using these, substitute ½ cup (finely chopped) chives.

Beef Teriyaki

Serves 4

4 × 200-g (7-oz) beef sirloin
  steaks, about 2.5 cm (1 in)
  thick

salt

1 tablespoon (20 ml/¾ fl oz)
  vegetable oil

⅓ cup (80 ml/3 fl oz) sake
  (Japanese rice wine)

3 tablespoons (60 ml/2 fl oz)
  mirin (sweet cooking wine)

2 tablespoons (40 ml/1½ fl oz)
  Japanese soy sauce

Sprinkle steaks lightly on both sides with salt.

Place oil in a heavy-based non-stick frying pan over high heat. Add the steaks and cook for 3 minutes, until underside is well browned. Turn meat over and brown the other side for 3 minutes. Reduce heat to medium–high, drizzle sake over the meat, then cover and cook for a further 2 minutes.

Remove steaks to a plate and reduce pan heat a little. Add the mirin and soy to the pan juices and cook for 1 minute or until sauce has reduced by half. Return meat to pan and turn in the sauce for about 15 seconds, just long enough to coat.

Transfer the meat to a cutting board and cut into 1-cm (⅜-in) slices. To serve, place slices on individual plates and then spoon over the remaining sauce from the pan.

Teriyaki Chicken

Serves 6

1 tablespoon (20 ml/¾ fl oz) vegetable oil

6 × 200-g (7-oz) chicken thigh fillets, skin on

TERIYAKI SAUCE

½ cup (125 ml/4 fl oz) sake (Japanese rice wine)

½ cup (125 ml/4 fl oz) mirin (sweet cooking wine)

½ cup (125 ml/4 fl oz) Japanese soy sauce

1 tablespoon (15 g/½ oz) caster sugar

First make the teriyaki sauce. Place all the ingredients in a small bowl and stir until sugar is dissolved, then set aside while you cook the chicken.

Heat oil in a large heavy-based non-stick frying pan over medium–high heat. Add the chicken pieces, skin side down, and cook for 3 minutes each side, or until golden brown all over.

Remove chicken, set aside, and drain off any excess fat from the pan. Add the teriyaki sauce to the pan and bring to the boil, then, as the sauce begins to thicken, return the chicken to the pan. Continue cooking, turning chicken pieces several times to coat evenly in the sauce. Cook for 1–2 minutes or until the sauce has reduced to a glaze.

Remove the chicken to a board and cut across into slices 1.5 cm (⅝ in) thick. Arrange slices, skin side up, on a plate and serve immediately.

Tofu with Spicy Pork

Mabo dofu

Serves 4

450 g (1 lb) firm silken tofu

250 g (9 oz) pork mince

⅓ cup (80 ml/3 fl oz) Japanese soy sauce

1 tablespoon (20 ml/¾ fl oz) sake (Japanese rice wine)

5 spring onions

1 tablespoon (20 ml/¾ fl oz) vegetable oil

2 teaspoons sesame oil

2 cloves garlic, crushed

1 tablespoon grated fresh ginger

1 tablespoon Chinese chilli paste (see note)

1 cup (250 ml/8½ fl oz) dashi stock II (page 35) or water

2 teaspoons caster sugar

1 tablespoon (15 g/½ oz) potato starch or cornflour

double quantity basic steamed rice (page 233), to serve (optional)

sansho pepper and sesame oil, for garnish

Wrap the tofu in a clean tea towel, place a dinner plate on top and set aside for 30 minutes to allow any excess moisture to be absorbed. Cut the tofu into 2.5-cm (1-in) pieces, and pat dry with paper towel.

Place pork in a bowl, sprinkle with 1 tablespoon (20 ml/¾ fl oz) soy sauce and half the sake, and leave to marinate for 10 minutes.

Slice three spring onions on the diagonal.

Heat both the oils in a heavy-based frying pan over medium heat. Add the spring onions and cook for 3 minutes, until softened. Add the garlic and ginger, and stir for 30–45 seconds until aromatic. Add the chilli paste and the pork mince, mix well to combine, then cook for 8–10 minutes or until the meat browns, stirring frequently. Add the tofu and stir gently to break up the pieces and mix in.

Add the dashi, sugar and remaining sake and soy, and bring to the boil. Mix the potato starch with a tablespoon of water to make a paste, then stir this into the meat mixture and combine well. Reduce heat to low and stir until the sauce thickens, then remove from the heat.

Spoon the pork mixture over rice, if using, or directly into a serving bowl. Finely slice remaining spring onions and scatter over. Sprinkle with sansho pepper and a drizzle of sesame oil, to taste. Serve immediately.

❀ This is a classic example of the Japanese interpreting another cuisine – the Sichuan flavours of the Chinese dish Mapo Dofu.

❀ Use a Sichuan chilli paste, available from Asian grocers.

Crumbed Sardines with Wasabi Mayonnaise

Serves 4 as a snack or light meal

12 butterflied sardines

⅓ cup (50 g/1¾ oz) plain flour

salt and ground white pepper, to season flour

1 egg

1½ cups panko (Japanese breadcrumbs)

vegetable oil for deep-frying

½ cup shiso (beefsteak plant) or basil leaves

sea salt and sansho pepper (optional)

WASABI MAYONNAISE

⅔ cup Japanese mayonnaise

½ teaspoon wasabi paste, or to taste

1 spring onion (white part only), finely chopped

2 teaspoons freshly squeezed lemon or lime juice, or to taste

To make the wasabi mayonnaise, combine all the ingredients in a bowl and mix well. Adjust seasoning to taste, adding extra wasabi or lemon juice if desired. Cover, and refrigerate until needed (use within 2 days).

Gently pat the sardines dry with paper towel. Sift the flour, salt and white pepper into a shallow wide bowl. In another bowl, lightly whisk the egg with 2 teaspoons water. Place the breadcrumbs on a plate. Dip each sardine in the flour, coating both sides evenly, then shake off any excess.

Next, dip sardines into the egg mixture to coat evenly, then shake a little to allow any excess to drip off. Last, dip sardines into the breadcrumbs and coat well. Place crumbed sardines on a plate and refrigerate while heating the oil.

Pour oil into a deep-fryer, wok or large saucepan to a depth of 5 cm (2 in) and heat to 180°C (360°F). The oil is ready when a piece of bread dropped into it rises instantly, surrounded by tiny bubbles, and turns golden brown.

Deep-fry the sardines, three at a time, for 2–3 minutes or until golden brown, crispy and cooked through. Remove, and drain well on crumpled paper towel. Between each batch, skim off any floating breadcrumbs from the surface of the oil.

Serve sardines immediately, scattered with shiso or basil leaves, and with a sprinkle of salt or sansho pepper if desired. Accompany with small bowls of wasabi mayonnaise for each person.

❁ Many fishmongers sell butterflied (boned, opened out and flattened) sardines. If preferred, replace the sardines with 12 raw (green) king prawns or scallops, or a combination of seafood.

Fried Pork Cutlet

Tonkatsu

Serves 4

600 g (1 lb 5 oz) pork fillet

½ cup (75 g/2½ oz) plain flour

salt and ground white pepper

2 eggs, lightly beaten

2 cups panko (Japanese breadcrumbs) or dried white breadcrumbs

vegetable oil for deep-frying

⅓ cup (80 ml/3 fl oz) sesame oil

1 lemon, cut into wedges

2 cups finely shredded white cabbage

wasabi paste, to serve

TONKATSU SAUCE

3 tablespoons (60 ml/2 fl oz) Worcestershire sauce

2 tablespoons (40 ml/1½ fl oz) Japanese soy sauce

3 tablespoons (60 ml/2 fl oz) tomato sauce

1 clove garlic, crushed

To make the tonkatsu sauce, combine all ingredients in a small saucepan over high heat and bring to the boil. Lower heat and simmer for 5 minutes, or until reduced by a third. Remove from heat and set aside to cool.

Cut pork fillet into 1-cm (⅜-in) slices. Using a meat mallet or rolling pin, pound each slice to flatten to 5 mm (¼ in) thick. Score edges of each slice in four or five places, to prevent the meat curling up while cooking. >

Have ready a plate of flour seasoned with salt and white pepper, a shallow bowl with the beaten eggs and another with the breadcrumbs. Lightly coat the pork pieces in seasoned flour, shaking off any excess. Dip the pieces into the egg, allowing any excess egg to drip off, and then coat evenly in the breadcrumbs. Place crumbed pork in a single layer on a plate and refrigerate while heating oil.

Pour oils into a deep-fryer, wok or large saucepan to a depth of 5 cm (2 in) and heat to 180°C (360°F). The oil is ready when a piece of bread dropped into it rises instantly, surrounded by tiny bubbles, and turns golden brown.

Deep-fry the crumbed pork in batches, two or three pieces at a time. Cook for 2–3 minutes, turn, and cook for a further 2 minutes until golden brown all over and pork is cooked through. Drain on paper towel and keep warm in a 100°C (210°F) oven. In between batches, skim the surface of the oil to remove any floating breadcrumbs.

Slice each piece of pork on the diagonal into 2-cm (¾-in) strips and serve accompanied with lemon wedges, shredded cabbage and wasabi, with the tonkatsu sauce for dipping.

Teriyaki Patties

Makes 8 (serves 4 as a main)

100 g (3½ oz) firm silken tofu

½ cup panko (Japanese breadcrumbs) or dried white breadcrumbs

400 g (14 oz) beef mince

200 g (7 oz) pork mince

1 small onion, finely chopped

1 clove garlic, crushed

1 egg, lightly beaten

3 tablespoons (60 ml/2 fl oz) teriyaki sauce (page 150), plus extra to serve

½ teaspoon salt

ground white pepper

1 tablespoon (20 ml/¾ fl oz) vegetable oil

Pat tofu dry with paper towel to remove excess moisture. Place in a bowl and mash with a fork, then stir in the breadcrumbs and set aside for 10 minutes until all the moisture is absorbed.

In a large bowl, combine the beef, pork, onion, garlic, egg, teriyaki sauce and breadcrumb mixture. Season with the salt and pepper to taste, and mix thoroughly. Divide mixture into eight portions and shape into patties. Place on a plate, cover, and refrigerate for an hour to firm up.

Heat oil in a large non-stick frying pan over medium–high heat. Cook patties in two batches, for about 7 minutes on each side or until cooked through.

Serve with salad and extra teriyaki sauce.

Tempura

Serves 4

2 quantities tempura batter (page 239)

8 raw (green) king prawns, shelled and deveined but tails left intact

1 small squid tube, about 20 cm (8 in) long, cleaned and tube opened out flat

4 whiting fillets, cut in half lengthways

4 fresh shiitake mushrooms, stems discarded

1 red capsicum, cut lengthways into eight slices

1 Asian eggplant, sliced into rounds 5 mm (¼ in) thick

1 small sweet potato, cut into rounds 5 mm (¼ in) thick

vegetable oil for deep-frying

plain flour, for coating

a 5-cm (2-in) piece daikon, peeled and finely grated, to serve

TEMPURA DIPPING SAUCE

300 ml (10 fl oz) dashi stock I (page 34)

3 tablespoons (60 ml/2 fl oz) mirin (sweet cooking wine)

1 tablespoon (15 g/½ oz) caster sugar

⅓ cup (80 ml/3 fl oz) Japanese soy sauce

Tempura batter should be prepared just before use, in small quantities as required. When cooking large quantities of ingredients, as here, only prepare a new batch when the first mixture is used up. >

Cut three shallow incisions across the belly (underside) of each prawn, to prevent them curling as they cook, then gently press the prawns out to straighten. Lightly score the underside of the squid in a criss-cross pattern, then cut into 5-cm (2-in) squares.

Arrange the prepared seafood and vegetables on separate plates, cover, and refrigerate until needed.

To prepare dipping sauce, place all the ingredients in a small saucepan over medium–high heat. Stir to dissolve sugar, then bring to the boil. Turn off the heat and keep warm.

Pour oil into a deep-fryer, deep wok or heavy-based saucepan to a depth of 7 cm (3 in) and heat to 180°C (360°F). The oil is ready when a drop of batter instantly rises to the surface, surrounded by tiny bubbles.

Have ready a bowl each of flour and batter. Dip each ingredient in the flour (which ensures the ingredients are dry, so the batter will stick well), shaking off any excess. Starting with the vegetables, dip each floured ingredient into the batter and shake a little so excess batter drips off, then slide into the oil a few pieces at a time. Deep-fry for 3 minutes or until golden brown, crispy and cooked through. Remove, and drain well on crumpled paper towel. Repeat with the remaining vegetables, skimming the surface of the oil between each batch to remove any leftover batter.

Now prepare the second mixture of batter and repeat battering process with the seafood. Deep-fry the fish and squid for 1–2 minutes and the prawns for 2–3 minutes or until just cooked through.

Pour the warm dipping sauce into small serving bowls. Serve the tempura with grated daikon and dipping sauce alongside. Tempura is best served immediately, but it can be kept warm in a 120°C (250°F) oven for 5 minutes.

Rare Beef Salad with Ponzu Sauce

Tataki

Serves 4 as a starter

4 × 180-g (6½-oz) beef fillet
(eye or scotch) steaks

salt and ground black pepper

1 tablespoon (20 ml/¾ fl oz)
vegetable oil

1 medium-sized carrot,
finely grated

½ daikon, peeled and
finely grated

2 tablespoons shredded shiso
(beefsteak plant) leaves

1½ cups (375 ml/12½ fl oz)
ponzu sauce (page 237),
to serve

wasabi paste, to serve

2 teaspoons finely grated fresh
ginger

Season the steaks on each side with salt and pepper.

Heat the oil in a heavy-based frying pan or grill pan over high heat. Cook the steaks for 2–3 minutes on each side (for rare). Drain on paper towel. Leave to rest for 15 minutes.

Cut each steak across the grain into very thin slices and arrange on individual plates. Combine the grated carrot and daikon, and place some on top of each serving, then scatter with the shiso. Give each person a small bowl of ponzu sauce and mounds of wasabi and ginger to dip their beef into.

❀ You can also use fresh tuna to make tataki, using 4 × 180-g (6½–oz) sashimi-grade tuna steaks. Cook as for the beef, making sure not to overcook as the fish should be rare.

Deep-fried Tofu

Agedashi-dofu

Serves 4 as a starter

600 g (1 lb 5 oz) firm silken tofu

vegetable or sunflower oil for deep-frying

⅓ cup (40 g/1½ oz) potato starch

DIPPING SAUCE

1 cup (250 ml/8½ fl oz) dashi stock I (page 34)

1 tablespoon (20 ml/¾ fl oz) mirin (sweet cooking wine)

1 tablespoon (20 ml/¾ fl oz) Japanese soy sauce

GARNISHES

a 5-cm (2-in) piece daikon, peeled and finely grated, and excess moisture squeezed out

2 tablespoons finely diced spring onions

dried bonito flakes

shredded nori

Wrap the tofu in a clean tea towel. Place a dinner plate on top and set aside for 30 minutes to allow any excess moisture to be absorbed. Cut the tofu into eight equal portions and pat dry with paper towel.

Meanwhile, make the dipping sauce. Combine the dashi, mirin and soy in a small saucepan over medium heat and bring to a simmer. Remove from heat and set aside.

Pour oil into a deep-fryer, wok or large saucepan to a depth of 5 cm (2 in) and heat to 180°C (360°F). The oil is ready when a piece of bread dropped into it rises instantly, surrounded by tiny bubbles, and turns golden brown.

Roll tofu in the potato starch to coat lightly and evenly on all sides. Deep-fry the tofu in two or three batches, for about 3–4 minutes or until pale golden. Working quickly, remove tofu from pan and drain well on paper towel. Divide between four small shallow bowls, place a small mound of grated daikon and diced spring onion on top and carefully pour a little of the (still warm) sauce into each bowl.

Serve immediately. Pass around bonito flakes and shredded nori for sprinkling, if desired.

- Chinese tofu is firmer and easier to handle than the Japanese variety.
- Shredded nori is available from Asian grocers, or you can cut nori sheets into fine shreds using scissors.

Pork Spring Rolls

Harumaki

Makes 12

4 dried shiitake mushrooms

30 g (1 oz) harusame noodles

1 cup bean sprouts, roughly chopped

⅓ cup canned bamboo shoots, drained and finely chopped

150 g (5 oz) pork mince

3 spring onions, finely sliced

2 teaspoons finely grated fresh ginger

2 tablespoons (40 ml/1½ fl oz) sake (Japanese rice wine)

1 teaspoon sesame oil

1½ tablespoons (30 ml/1 fl oz) Japanese soy sauce

1 teaspoon caster sugar

salt and ground white pepper

3 tablespoons (45 g/1½ oz) potato starch or cornflour

12 spring-roll wrappers

vegetable oil for deep-frying

combination soy sauce (page 236), to serve

Soak the mushrooms in warm water for 30 minutes, to soften. Drain, then discard the stems and cut the caps into thin slices.

Soak the noodles in warm water for 10 minutes. Drain well, squeeze out any excess water, then cut into 5-cm (2-in) lengths.

Place noodles in a bowl and add bean sprouts, mushrooms, bamboo shoots, pork, spring onions, ginger, sake, sesame oil, soy sauce and sugar, and season with salt and white pepper. Mix to combine, then sprinkle with 2 tablespoons of the potato starch and mix again to combine well. >

Mix the remaining potato starch with a tablespoon of water to form a paste. Lay out the spring-roll wrappers on a clean work surface. Place about a tablespoonful of the pork mixture across one corner of a wrapper. Fold the corner over the filling, then fold both sides in and roll up to form a log. Seal the edges with a little of the flour paste. Repeat the process with the remaining wrappers and filling.

Pour oil into a deep-fryer, wok or large saucepan to a depth of 5 cm (2 in) and heat to 170°C (340°F). The oil is ready when a piece of bread dropped into it rises instantly, surrounded by tiny bubbles, and turns golden brown. Deep-fry three or four spring rolls at a time, for about 8 minutes or until golden and cooked through. Drain on paper towel and keep warm in a low (100°C/210°F) oven while you cook the remaining spring rolls.

Serve hot, with the dipping sauce.

❀ Dried or frozen spring-roll wrappers are available from Asian food stores.

❀ If harusame noodles are not available, substitute with cellophane mung bean noodles (available at Asian supermarkets).

Chicken Marinated & Deep-fried

Tatsuta-age

Serves 6–8 as a starter

⅓ cup (80 ml/3 fl oz) Japanese
soy sauce

3 tablespoons (60 ml/2 fl oz)
mirin (sweet cooking wine)

1 tablespoon (20 ml/¾ fl oz)
sake (Japanese rice wine)

2 teaspoons ginger juice
(see note page 47)

900 g (2 lb) chicken thigh or
breast fillets, skin on

vegetable or sunflower oil
for deep-frying

about ½ cup (85 g/3 oz)
cornflour, for coating

2 teaspoons nori flakes

sea salt and sansho pepper
(optional)

Japanese mayonnaise and
lemon wedges, to serve

Make the marinade by combining the soy, mirin, sake and ginger juice in a ceramic or glass dish. Cut the chicken into 4-cm (1½-in) pieces, place in marinade and toss to coat well. Cover, and refrigerate for an hour.

Fill a deep-fryer or heavy-based saucepan with vegetable oil to a depth of 7 cm (2½ in) and heat to 180°C (360°F). The oil is ready when a piece of bread dropped into it rises instantly and turns golden brown.

Combine the cornflour with the nori flakes in a shallow bowl. Using a sieve, drain the chicken and discard any excess marinade. In batches, toss the pieces in the flour to coat lightly and evenly, dusting off any excess. >

Deep-fry the chicken in batches, for 3–5 minutes until golden brown and cooked through. Skim the surface of the oil between each batch to remove any floating fragments. Drain fried pieces well on paper towel and keep warm in a low (100°C/210°F) oven while cooking the remaining pieces.

Serve immediately, sprinkled with salt and sansho if desired, and accompanied with mayonnaise and lemon wedges. (It is delicious served in iceberg-lettuce cups and topped with a dollop of the mayonnaise.)

Simmered, Steamed & One-pot Dishes

Simmering (nimono) is a common Japanese cooking method. The stock, which includes dashi, mirin, sake, soy and miso in different combinations, imparts delicate flavour to the food. A special 'drop-lid' (otoshi-buta), which fits inside the pan and covers the ingredients, is traditionally used to ensure all the food is submerged in the stock. In a western kitchen a circle of baking paper will suffice.

Steaming (mushimono) is perfect for quick-cooking the freshest ingredients, so maintaining their texture and colour. It is best to steam small amounts and make sure the steamer is very hot and steaming vigorously before you add the food.

One-pot cooking, known as nabemono, is a convivial eating experience for a party. A flameproof casserole (donabe) filled with simmering stock, or a frying pan, is placed on a portable hotplate in the centre of the table, and diners cook the prepared vegetables or meat themselves.

< Chicken, Parsley & Wasabi Salad (page 176)

Chicken, Parsley & Wasabi Salad

Toriwasa

Serves 4

1 skinless chicken breast fillet,
trimmed of fat

⅓ cup (80 ml/3 fl oz) sake
(Japanese rice wine)

salt

4 cups flat-leaf parsley
(leaves only)

2 tablespoons (40 ml/1½ fl oz)
Japanese soy sauce

1 tablespoon finely grated
fresh wasabi (or 2 teaspoons
wasabi paste)

Cut the chicken breast across the grain into very thin slices, then cut each slice into strips. Place chicken, sake and a pinch of salt in a small saucepan over medium heat. Bring to the boil, then immediately turn off heat and set aside to cool (in the sake) to room temperature.

Bring a small saucepan of lightly salted water to the boil, add the parsley and cook for 1 minute. Drain, and plunge into a bowl of iced water to stop the cooking process, then drain again. Squeeze out any excess water, pat leaves dry with paper towel and then chop coarsely.

Add the parsley and soy sauce to the chicken and sake, and stir gently to combine. To serve, divide salad into small serving bowls and top each with 1 teaspoon fresh wasabi or ½ teaspoon wasabi paste.

Shabu-shabu

Serves 6

750 g (1 lb 10 oz) beef sirloin, trimmed

a 10-cm (4-in) length of kombu (kelp)

100 g (3½ oz) harusame noodles (see note page 170)

1 carrot, sliced very thinly

6 button mushrooms, stems trimmed and caps wiped

9 spring onions

6 fresh shiitake mushrooms, stems discarded

300 g (10½ oz) firm tofu, cut into 6 equal pieces

18 gingko nuts (see note page 178)

100 g (3½ oz) canned bamboo shoots, drained and thinly sliced

¼ Chinese cabbage, cut across into 2.5-cm (1-in) slices

1 quantity sesame-seed sauce (page 234)

1 daikon, peeled and finely grated

½ quantity ponzu sauce (page 237)

You will need a portable electric or gas hotplate for this dish.

Place beef in the freezer for an hour or until partially frozen, then slice (across the grain) very thinly. Arrange slices on a platter.

Three-quarters-fill a large flameproof casserole with water and add the piece of kombu. Set aside while you prepare the other ingredients. >

Soak the harusame noodles in a bowl of warm water for 10 minutes to soften. Drain, and place noodles in a bowl. Blanch the carrot, and drain.

Cut a cross in the top of each button mushroom cap. Cut six of the spring onions into 4-cm (1½-in) lengths. Arrange the mushrooms, tofu, gingko nuts, bamboo shoots, cabbage, spring onion lengths and carrot decoratively on a second platter. Finely chop the remaining spring onions and stir into the sesame-seed sauce. Stir the daikon into the ponzu sauce. Then place the sauces in small bowls for each person.

Place portable hotplate on the dining table. Put the casserole over a high heat, bring to the boil (remove the kombu just before the water reaches boiling point), then reduce to a rolling simmer.

At this point each person can use chopsticks to help themselves to ingredients and dip them into the broth to poach (a few seconds for the beef, and a few minutes for the vegetables). As diners remove food from the pot, they dip it into their sauce of choice and eat immediately. Skim the surface of the broth from time to time, to remove any rising scum.

* The name shabu-shabu refers to the swishing sound of the chopsticks in the broth.
* Gingko nuts are available frozen or vacuum packed in Asian food stores.

Poached Pork Fillet

Serves 4

600 g (1 lb 5 oz) pork fillet

1.5 L (3 pt 3 fl oz) dashi
stock II (page 35)

3 tablespoons (60 ml/2 fl oz)
Japanese soy sauce

a 10-cm (4-in) piece fresh
ginger, thinly sliced

2 spring onions, thinly sliced

Japanese mustard, to serve

Tie the pork with string to maintain its shape during cooking.

Place the dashi in a large saucepan and bring to boil. Add the soy sauce, ginger and spring onions, then add the pork and reduce heat to a simmer. Cook for 30 minutes, until meat is cooked through and tender. Remove saucepan from heat and leave the pork in the stock for 20 minutes to cool. Remove pork from the liquid and cut into 1-cm (⅜-in) slices. Serve with Japanese mustard.

The pork can also be served cold. To do this, place poached pork in a clean bowl and pour the cooking liquid over it through a strainer. Cover, and refrigerate overnight or until chilled. Remove the pork and discard cooking liquor, slice the pork as above, and serve with the mustard.

❀ A nashi and celery salad (page 74) goes well with this dish.

Beef Sukiyaki

Serves 6

650 g (1 lb 8 oz) beef eye or scotch fillet, trimmed

250 g (9 oz) shirataki noodles

4 spring onions, cut on the diagonal into 1.5 cm (⅝-in) lengths

6 fresh shiitake mushrooms, stems discarded, and a cross cut into top of each cap

¼ cup chopped Chinese cabbage

½ cup mitsuba (Japanese parsley) or flat-leaf parsley leaves 300 g (10½ oz) firm tofu, cut into 6 equal pieces

a 3-cm (1¼-in) piece beef fat or 1 tablespoon (20 ml/¾ fl oz) vegetable oil

6 eggs (optional)

basic steamed rice (page 233), to serve

SAUCE

2 cups (500 ml/17 fl oz) dashi stock II (page 35)

⅔ cup (160 ml/5½ fl oz) Japanese soy sauce

2 tablespoons (40 ml/1½ fl oz) sake (Japanese rice wine)

2 tablespoons (30 g/1 oz) caster sugar

You will need a portable electric or gas hotplate (or an electric frypan) for this dish.

To make the sauce, place the dashi, soy sauce, sake and sugar in a small saucepan over medium heat. Stir to dissolve sugar, bring to a simmer and then remove from heat. Transfer to a jug and set aside. >

Place beef in freezer for an hour or until partially frozen, then slice very thinly. Arrange slices on a large platter, leaving room for other ingredients.

Soak the noodles in a bowl of warm water for 5 minutes. Drain well, and then cut into 15-cm (6-in) lengths. Arrange decoratively on the platter along with the vegetables and tofu.

Put portable hotplate on the dining table. Put a heavy-based frying pan over high heat. Add the beef fat (or vegetable oil), and rub over the base to grease the pan. Cooking in batches, add about one-third of both the spring onions and the beef slices, and quickly stir-fry until brown. Push meat to the side (and remove beef fat, if used). Add a selection of the remaining ingredients, and enough of the sauce to cover. Stir and cook for 3–4 minutes until ingredients are tender and warmed through.

Give each guest a bowl, into which they break an egg (if desired) and lightly beat it with chopsticks. They then help themselves to the cooked ingredients and dip them into the egg – it will cook in the residual heat of the ingredients. As the pan empties, repeat the cooking process (add more spring onions and beef, followed by the remaining ingredients). Add water, if needed, to prevent the flavours of the sauce becoming too concentrated. Serve with rice.

🌸 For the beef fat, just ask your butcher for some trimmings.

Seafood Sukiyaki

Uosuki

Serves 4

¼ Chinese cabbage, cut into slices 2 cm (¾ in) thick

4 large raw (green) prawns, shelled and deveined but tails left intact and heads reserved

4 scallops, removed from shell

4 oysters, removed from shell

4 mussels, removed from shell

1 small crab (sand or blue), cleaned (ask fishmonger to do this for you)

2 snapper fillets (about 200 g/ 7 oz each), cut into slices 1 cm (⅜ in) thick

200 g (7 oz) firm tofu, drained and cut into 4 equal pieces

4 spring onions, cut into 5-cm (2-in) lengths

4 small eggs (optional)

COOKING STOCK

1 cup (250 ml/8½ fl oz) dashi stock I (page 34)

⅓ cup (80 ml/3 fl oz) Japanese soy sauce

2 tablespoons (40 ml/1½ fl oz) mirin (sweet cooking wine)

1 tablespoon (20 ml/¾ fl oz) sake (Japanese rice wine)

1 tablespoon (15 g/½ oz) caster sugar

Bring a saucepan of water to the boil, add the cabbage and cook for 1 minute. Drain, and plunge into a bowl of cold water to stop cooking process. Drain again.

Prepare the cooking stock by combining the ingredients and stirring to dissolve the sugar. >

Carefully arrange the seafood (including the prawn heads), tofu and spring onions in a large, heavy flameproof casserole. Pour in the prepared cooking stock and place the pot over medium–high heat. Cover, bring to a simmer and cook for 10–12 minutes or until the seafood is tender, skimming away any rising scum on the surface. Remove and discard prawn heads.

Serve at the table, directly from the pot. To eat, each person can lightly beat an egg (if desired), in their bowl and then add their choice of ingredients from the pot, with some stock: the egg cooks from the heat of the ingredients.

You can substitute another firm-fleshed white fish for the snapper, such as flathead or barramundi.

Oysters in Miso

Kaki-miso

Serves 6 as a starter

8 spring onions, tops trimmed

600 g (1 lb 5 oz) freshly
shelled oysters, rinsed
in cold water

100 g (3½ oz) brown-rice miso

¼ cup (55 g/2 oz) caster sugar

3 tablespoons (60 ml/2 fl oz)
Japanese rice vinegar

Bring a medium-sized saucepan of lightly salted water to the boil. Drop in spring onions and leave for about 15 seconds, until just wilted. Remove with a slotted spoon and plunge into a bowl of iced water to stop the cooking process. Remove, pat dry with paper towel and cut into 2.5-cm (1-in) lengths.

Bring water back to the boil and plunge the oysters in for 30 seconds. Remove, and put straight into a bowl of iced water to stop the cooking process. Drain well.

Combine the miso, sugar and vinegar in a small saucepan over a low–medium heat, stirring with a wooden spoon until sugar dissolves. Add the oysters and cook for about 1 minute to warm through. Remove saucepan from the heat, then gently stir in the spring onions.

Serve warm or at room temperature.

Simmered Baby Fish

Serves 2

2 baby snapper or flounder
(or other firm-fleshed white
fish), about 300 g (10½ oz)
each, cleaned

⅓ cup (80 ml/3 fl oz) sake
(Japanese rice wine)

⅓ cup (80 ml/3 fl oz) mirin
(sweet cooking wine)

¾ cup (180 ml/6 fl oz) dashi
stock II (page 35)

½ cup (125 ml/4 fl oz)
Japanese soy sauce

pinch of caster sugar

a 5-cm (2-in) length daikon,
cut into matchsticks

Rinse fish under cold running water and pat dry with paper towel. Cut three diagonal slashes about 5 mm (¼ in) deep on one side of the fish (bearing in mind that the head of the fish traditionally faces left when served).

Place the sake, mirin, dashi, soy and sugar in a deep-sided frying pan large enough to hold both fish. Bring to the boil over high heat, then slide the fish into the pan, cut side up. Spoon some sauce over the fish and bring back to the boil. Cover with a piece of baking paper that just fits inside the frying pan, reduce heat to medium and cook for 7–8 minutes or until the flesh is opaque. Remove the paper and use a wide spatula to carefully lift the fish onto individual plates.

To serve, spoon remaining sauce over the fish. Serve daikon in a bowl to pass around.

Vegetable Hotpot

Serves 4

1 tablespoon (20 ml/¾ fl oz) vegetable oil

2 teaspoons sesame oil

4 baby leeks (white parts only), cut into 4-cm (1½-in) lengths

1 large carrot, cut into 1.5-cm (⅝-in) slices

100 g (3½ oz) lotus root, cut into 5-mm (¼-in) slices

a 2-cm (¾ in) piece fresh ginger, cut into matchsticks

½ cup canned sliced bamboo shoots, drained and rinsed

4 fresh shiitake mushrooms, stems discarded and caps quartered

2 cups (500 ml/17 fl oz) dashi stock II (page 35)

⅓ cup (80 ml/3 fl oz) Japanese soy sauce

3 tablespoons (60 ml/2 fl oz) mirin (sweet cooking wine)

1 tablespoon (15 g/½ oz) caster sugar

50 g enoki mushrooms, split into 4 bunches

100 g (3½ oz) mizuna or spinach leaves, roughly chopped

basic steamed rice (page 233), to serve

Heat both the oils in a large saucepan over a medium–high heat. Add the leeks and cook for 2 minutes. Add the carrot and lotus root, and cook for another 2–3 minutes or until lightly golden. Add the ginger, bamboo shoots and shiitake mushrooms, and cook for 2 minutes more.

Add the dashi, soy, mirin and sugar to the pan and bring to a boil, then reduce heat and simmer for 12–15 minutes, or until the vegetables are just tender. Add the enoki mushrooms and the mizuna or spinach, and cook for 1 minute or until spinach has just wilted.

Serve in deep bowls, with rice.

Sweet Braised Pork

Butano kakani

Serves 6–8 as a starter

1 tablespoon (20 ml/¾ fl oz)
vegetable oil

900 g (2 lb) boneless pork belly,
cut into 5-cm (2-in) cubes

a 5-cm (2-in) piece fresh ginger,
thinly sliced

1 spring onion, cut into 5-cm
(2-in) lengths

1 cup (250 ml/8½ fl oz) dashi
stock II (page 35)

½ cup (125 ml/4 fl oz) sake
(Japanese rice wine)

3 tablespoons (60 ml/2 fl oz)
mirin (sweet cooking wine)

½ cup (125 ml/4 fl oz)
Japanese soy sauce

⅓ cup (60 g/2 oz) soft brown
sugar

Heat the oil in a large frying pan over medium–high heat. Add the pork and cook for 5 minutes to brown pieces all over. Remove from pan, and drain on paper towel.

Place pork, ginger, spring onion and 1 L (34 fl oz) water in a large saucepan and bring to the boil over high heat. Then reduce the heat to a simmer and cook for 2 hours, adding extra water if needed to keep the pork covered in liquid. Remove and drain pork, and discard the ginger and spring onion.

Put the dashi, sake, mirin, soy sauce, sugar and 250 ml (8½ fl oz) water into a clean saucepan over high heat and bring to the boil, stirring to dissolve the sugar. Add the drained pork, return to the boil, then reduce heat to a low simmer. Place a drop-lid or circle of baking paper over the ingredients to keep them covered and simmer the pork for 1 hour until the liquid has reduced to a thick syrup and pork is very tender.

Serve warm, as one of several starters, or as a main with rice and greens.

Simmered Tofu

Yudofu

Serves 6 as a side dish or starter

a 10-cm (4-in) length kombu
(kelp), wiped with a damp
cloth

600 g (1 lb 5 oz) firm silken
tofu

GARNISHES

4 spring onions, finely sliced

1 sheet toasted nori, cut into
fine shreds

a 5-cm (2-in) piece fresh
ginger, finely grated

dried bonito flakes

SAUCE

2 cups (500 ml/17 fl oz) dashi
stock II (page 35)

½ cup (125 ml/4 fl oz)
Japanese soy sauce

2 tablespoons (40 ml/1½ fl oz)
mirin (sweet cooking wine)

⅓ cup dried bonito flakes

Score the surface of the kombu with a knife, to help release its flavour.
Place kombu and 1.5 L (3 pt 3 fl oz) cold water in a large saucepan and set
aside to soak for an hour.

Meanwhile prepare the garnishes and divide between small individual
bowls. >

To make the sauce, place the dashi, soy and mirin in a saucepan and bring to the boil. Add the bonito flakes, then remove from the heat at once. When the bonito flakes have settled to the bottom of the pan, strain the liquid into another saucepan and keep warm over a low heat.

Cut tofu into 12 equal pieces. Bring kombu water to a simmer over medium–high heat, then remove kombu with a slotted spoon and discard. Gently immerse the tofu pieces and cook for 2 minutes or until heated through. (Make sure the heat is not too high or the tofu will become dry and tough.) Carefully remove the tofu with a slotted spoon and transfer to individual bowls. Discard cooking liquid.

Pour warmed sauce into a jug. To serve, pass around sauce for guests to pour over the tofu. Diners add garnishes to taste.

❀ This a great dish to heat and serve at the table using a portable electric or gas hotplate, so guests can enjoy the whole cooking process.

Soba-noodle Broth

Serves 4

400 g (14 oz) dried soba
noodles

2 L (4 pt 4 fl oz) dashi stock II
(page 35)

½ cup (125 ml/4 fl oz)
Japanese soy sauce

2 tablespoons (40 ml/1½ fl oz)
mirin (sweet cooking wine)

1 tablespoon (15 g/½ oz) caster
sugar

2 spring onions (white parts
only), thinly sliced on the
diagonal

Two-thirds-fill a large saucepan with lightly salted water and bring to the boil. Add the noodles gradually, separating them so they don't stick together. Bring water back to the boil, add 1 cup (250 ml/8½ fl oz) cold water and allow water to return to the boil again. Add another cup of cold water and cook until water returns to the boil once more, or until the noodles are just cooked. Drain the noodles, rinse under cold water to remove excess starch, and drain well again.

Meanwhile prepare a broth by combining the dashi, soy, mirin and sugar in a saucepan over medium–high heat. Stir to dissolve sugar, bring to the boil, then reduce to a simmer and cook for 15 minutes (uncovered).

Divide noodles between four soup bowls and ladle the broth over. Sprinkle with the spring onions and serve immediately.

Salmon & Tofu Hotpot

Ishi kari-nabe

Serves 4

12 dried shiitake mushrooms

2 L (4 pt 4 fl oz) dashi stock II (page 35)

⅓ cup (80 ml/3 fl oz) Japanese soy sauce

3 tablespoons (60 ml/2 fl oz) mirin (sweet cooking wine)

2 tablespoons (40 ml/1½ fl oz) sake (Japanese rice wine)

400 g (14 oz) Japanese pumpkin (kabocha), peeled and cut into 2.5-cm (1-in) chunks

3 spring onions, cut into 5-cm (2-in) lengths

½ small Chinese cabbage, cut into 5-cm (2-in) thick slices

500 g (1 lb 2 oz) salmon fillet, cut into 5-cm (2-in) chunks

500 g (1 lb 2 oz) grilled tofu, cut into 8 pieces

ponzu sauce (page 237) and sesame-seed sauce (page 234), to serve

Soak the mushrooms in warm water for 30 minutes. Drain, discard stems and slice caps thinly.

Place the dashi, soy, mirin and sake in a large, heavy-based flameproof casserole and bring to the boil over medium–high heat. Add the shiitake mushrooms and pumpkin, bring back to the boil and cook for 15 minutes or until pumpkin is just tender. Add the spring onions and cabbage, and simmer for 2 minutes.

Add the salmon to the casserole, bring back to a simmer and cook for 5 minutes. Carefully add the tofu and cook for a further 3 minutes or until the salmon is just cooked through.

Serve the hotpot at the table. Guest can serve themselves and add sauces to taste.

✿ You can buy ready-grilled tofu (yaki tofu) at Asian food stores. Alternatively, use firm silken tofu.

Beef & Potato Stew

Nikujaga

Serves 4

400 g (14 oz) beef sirloin steak

500 g (1 lb 2 oz) potatoes, peeled and cut into 3-cm (1¼-in) chunks

2 tablespoons (40 ml/1½ fl oz) vegetable oil

1 tablespoon (20 ml/¾ fl oz) sesame oil

1 large onion, cut into 6 wedges

2 cups (500 ml/17 fl oz) dashi stock II (page 35)

⅓ cup (80 ml/3 fl oz) Japanese soy sauce

2 tablespoons (30 g/1 oz) caster sugar

2 tablespoons (40 ml/1½ fl oz) mirin (sweet cooking wine)

1 tablespoon (20 ml/¾ fl oz) sake (Japanese rice wine)

Place beef in the freezer for 45 minutes or until partially frozen, then slice very finely. Soak potatoes in a bowl of cold water for 15 minutes, to remove excess starch. Drain, and pat dry with paper towel.

Combine the vegetable and sesame oils and heat two-thirds of the mixture in a large heavy-based saucepan over medium–high heat. Add the potatoes and stir-fry for 8–10 minutes, until lightly golden all over. Remove potatoes and set aside, then add the onions to the pan and cook for 3–5 minutes until softened. Remove onions and set aside. >

Heat the remaining oil in the saucepan. Cook the beef in two batches, stir-frying for 2–3 minutes until the meat turns brown. Return the potatoes, onions and all the beef to the saucepan, add the dashi, soy, sugar, mirin and sake, and bring to a boil. Reduce to a simmer, skim any rising scum from the surface, cover ingredients with a drop-lid or circle of baking paper, and cook for 40–45 minutes or until the potatoes are cooked through and meat is tender.

Adjust seasoning if needed with extra soy or sugar. Serve in bowls.

Rice & Green Peas

Serves 4 as a side dish

400 g (14 oz) Japanese short-
grain rice

2 cups (500 ml/17 fl oz) dashi
stock II (page 35)

1 teaspoon Japanese soy sauce

1 tablespoon (20 ml/¾ fl oz)
sake (Japanese rice wine)

225 g (8 oz) shelled peas

pinch of salt

Put the rice in a large bowl and rinse under cold water, swirling the rice around, until the water runs clear. Drain in a sieve and leave for 30 minutes.

Place rice, dashi, soy and sake in a medium-sized saucepan. Scatter peas over the surface of the rice, cover with a tight-fitting lid, set saucepan over medium heat and bring to the boil. (If using a rice cooker, follow the manufacturer's instructions.) Do not lift the lid to check the rice has come to the boil, as steam will escape: instead, listen for the sound of boiling and look for white scum bubbling up around the edge of the lid. At this point, reduce the heat to very low and leave the rice to simmer for 15 minutes. Remove from heat and set aside (lid on) for 10 minutes before using.

Gently mix the peas through the rice. Season with a little salt, if needed, and serve hot.

Steamed Snapper on Kombu

Serves 4

a 15-cm (6-in) square piece kombu (kelp), wiped with a damp cloth

2 × 250-g (9-oz) snapper fillets, skin on

salt

SAUCE

2 cups (500 ml/17 fl oz) dashi stock II (page 35)

1 tablespoon (20 ml/¾ fl oz) Japanese soy sauce

3 tablespoons (60 ml/3 fl oz) sake (Japanese rice wine)

1 tablespoon (15 g/½ oz) potato starch or cornflour

1 tablespoon (20 ml/¾ fl oz) ginger juice (see note page 47)

Soak kombu in a bowl of water for an hour.

Lightly sprinkle salt on both sides of the fish fillets, wrap in a clean damp tea towel, place on a plate and refrigerate for 1 hour. Rinse the fish under cold water to remove the salt, then pat dry with paper towel.

Cut each fish fillet crossways into 2.5-cm (1-in) slices. Make two shallow cuts across each piece (this prevents curling and reduces shrinkage during cooking). >

Place the drained kombu in the base of a wide shallow heatproof bowl large enough to hold the fish pieces. Arrange the fish, skin side down, on top, then seal the bowl tightly with foil. Bring a wok half-full of water to the boil and place a steaming rack or round wire cake rack over the water. (Depending on the diameter of your wok, the fish may need to be cooked in batches.) Place the bowl of fish on the rack, cover wok with a tight-fitting lid, and steam for 12 minutes.

To make the sauce, place the dashi, soy and sake in a small saucepan and bring to the boil, then reduce heat to a low simmer. Mix the potato starch with a tablespoon of the dashi mixture to form a paste, then stir this into the dashi mixture until combined and the sauce has thickened enough to coat the back of a spoon. Remove from the heat and stir in ginger juice, to taste.

Carefully transfer the fish to serving plates and spoon the sauce over. Serve with rice and steamed greens (such as green beans or broccoli).

One-pot Noodles

Nabeyaki udon

Serves 4

200 g (8 oz) spinach

800 g (1 lb 12 oz) fresh udon
noodles

1.5 L (3 pt 3 fl oz) dashi
stock II (page 35)

½ cup (125 ml/4½ oz)
Japanese soy sauce

3 tablespoons (60 ml/2 fl oz)
mirin (sweet cooking wine)

200 g (7 oz) chicken thigh
fillets, cut into 2-cm (¾-in)
pieces

2 spring onions, finely sliced

4 slices kamaboko (fish cake),
each about 5 mm (¼ in)
thick

1 quantity simmered shiitake
mushrooms (page 65),
thinly sliced (optional)

4 eggs

shichimi togarashi (seven-
spice mix), to serve

Bring a large saucepan of salted water to the boil, add the spinach and
cook for 1 minute until wilted. Using a slotted spoon remove leaves and
plunge into a bowl of cold water to stop the cooking process. Drain well,
gently squeeze out the excess water, then cut spinach mound into 2.5-cm
(1-in) pieces and set aside.

Bring the salted water back to the boil, add the noodles and cook for about
5 minutes (or according to packet instructions) until noodles are cooked
through. Turn off heat and allow noodles to stand for 5 minutes, drain, then
rinse under cold water to stop cooking process. Drain well again. >

Meanwhile, combine dashi, soy and mirin in a saucepan over medium–high heat, add chicken and bring just to the boil. Reduce to a simmer and cook for 5 minutes or until chicken is just cooked through (skim the surface of the cooking liquid to remove any rising scum). Add the noodles, spinach, spring onions, kamaboko and mushrooms, bring to a simmer, then immediately remove from the heat.

Working quickly, divide between four 2-cup (500-ml/17-fl oz) clay pots or deep bowls.

Using the back of a spoon, make a hollow in the centre of the noodle mixture in each dish. Crack an egg into the hollow, cover dish with a lid (or use a piece of aluminium foil and seal around edges), and leave for 5–6 minutes to steam the egg until just set. Serve immediately, with shichimi togarashi for sprinkling.

❁ Sometimes tempura prawns (page 160) are served with this dish, one arranged on top of each portion.

Hotpot

Oden

Serves 4

100 g (3½ oz) konnyaku, cut into 1.5-cm (½-in) cubes

1 L (34 fl oz) dashi stock II (page 35)

3 tablespoons (60 ml/2 fl oz) Japanese soy sauce

2 tablespoons (40 ml/1½ fl oz) sake (Japanese rice wine)

1 tablespoon (15 g/½ oz) caster sugar

a 5-cm (2-in) length daikon, peeled and cut into quarters lengthways

4 baby new (chat) potatoes, peeled

100 g (3½ oz) kamaboko (fish cake), cut into 1-cm (⅜-in) slices

4 small hard-boiled eggs, shelled

¼ cup canned sliced bamboo shoots, drained

300 g (10½ oz) deep-fried tofu (page 166), cut into four pieces

Bring a small saucepan of water to the boil. Add the konnyaku and boil for 1 minute, then drain well.

In a large saucepan, combine the dashi, soy, sake and sugar. Bring to the boil, add the konnyaku, daikon and potatoes, then reduce to a low simmer and cook (uncovered) for 1 hour. Add additional stock if required to keep the ingredients covered. Add the fish cake, eggs and bamboo shoots, bring back to a simmer and cook for a further 15 minutes to heat through.

Divide tofu between four large bowls, then ladle the stew over.

Chicken One-pot

Tori-mizutaki

Serves 6

1 × 1.3-kg (2 lb 4-oz) chicken

2 medium-sized carrots,
cut in half lengthways

6 fresh shiitake mushrooms,
stems discarded

a 10-cm (4-in) length kombu
(kelp)

300 g (10½ oz) Chinese
cabbage leaves, torn into
4-cm (1½-in) pieces

100 g (3½ oz) enoki
mushrooms

50 g (1¾ oz) fresh
chrysanthemum leaves
or watercress

300 g (10½ oz) firm tofu,
cut into 3-cm cubes

ACCOMPANIMENTS

½ quantity ponzu sauce
(page 237)

a 4-cm (1½-in) piece daikon,
peeled and grated

2 spring onions, finely
chopped

You will need a portable gas or electric hotplate for this dish.

Using a heavy cook's knife or cleaver, cut chicken into 5-cm (2-in) pieces, including bone and skin. Cut the carrot halves crossways into pieces 1 cm (⅜ in) wide. Cut a shallow cross into the top of each shiitake cap.

Place 1.5 L (3 pt 3 fl oz) cold water and the kombu in a large saucepan over high heat and bring to the boil, removing the kombu just before the water reaches boiling point. Add the chicken pieces and return to the boil, then reduce heat to a simmer.

Cook for 10 minutes, or until chicken pieces are just cooked through, then transfer chicken to a bowl and spoon a little of the cooking liquid over to keep it moist. Return stock to the boil, add carrots and cook for 2 minutes, then remove from pan and plunge into iced water to stop the cooking process.

Arrange all the vegetables, chrysanthemum leaves and tofu on a platter. Place the chicken on a separate platter.

Pour the stock through a fine mesh strainer into a flameproof casserole until about three-quarters full (reserve any excess stock, cover and refrigerate). Put the portable hotplate on the dining table. Provide a small dish of ponzu sauce for each person, as well as bowls of daikon and spring onions. Place casserole over medium–high heat and bring to a simmer, then add a selection of ingredients and cook for 3–5 minutes, or until just tender and heated through.

Each person removes their choice of simmered ingredients, dips them into the sauce and adds accompaniments.

❀ Chrysanthemum leaves are available at Asian food stores.

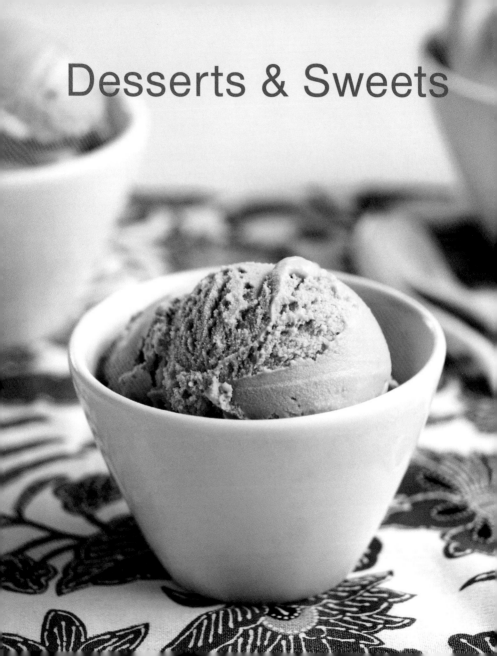

Desserts & Sweets

Traditionally, a Japanese meal ends with fresh fruit. The fruit should be seasonal and in perfect condition, presented attractively and appetisingly.

Japanese sweets, known as wa-gashi, are commonly served with tea, eaten as a snack, or given as gifts. There are many types of these confectioneries, such as cakes (namagashi), jellies (kanten), steamed filled dough balls, rice cakes (mochi) and hard sweets (higashi). These popular sweets are colourful, artful creations with surprising nutritional value. Protein packed and high in fibre, azuki beans are a common ingredient, as are soybeans, rice flour and sesame seeds.

Western-style desserts and sweets have become increasingly popular. Some of the recipes in the following pages are traditional, while others combine favourite western desserts with Japanese flavours.

< Green Tea Ice-cream (page 212)

Green Tea Ice-cream

Makes 1 L (34 fl oz)

2 cups (500 ml/17 fl oz)
full-cream milk

2 cups (500 ml/17 fl oz) cream

1 vanilla pod, split in half
lengthways

8 egg yolks

⅔ cup (145 g/5 oz) caster
sugar

1 tablespoon matcha
(green-tea powder)

Reserve ¼ cup (60 ml/2 fl oz) of the milk. Combine the remaining milk with the cream and the vanilla pod in a heavy-based saucepan over medium heat and bring to a simmer (don't let it boil). Remove from heat and allow the vanilla to infuse for 10 minutes, then remove pod and reserve.

Meanwhile, whisk the egg yolks and sugar until light and creamy. Gradually pour in the hot milk mixture, whisking continuously until incorporated.

Pour the mixture into a clean saucepan and place over low–medium heat. Stir constantly with a wooden spoon for 6–8 minutes or until the mixture thickens and coats the back of the spoon. Remove from the heat, then pour custard through a strainer into a clean glass or ceramic bowl. Scrape seeds from half the vanilla pod into the strained custard, then discard pod.

Stir the green-tea powder into the reserved milk to form a paste, then stir this into the custard and combine well. Cover the surface of the custard with cling wrap, leave to cool for 10 minutes, then refrigerate overnight or until completely chilled.

Churn custard in an ice-cream maker, following the manufacturer's instructions, then transfer to an airtight container and place in freezer until required. Homemade ice-cream is best served soon after it's made.

Powdered green tea is available at Asian food stores.

Honeydew Melon
with Midori Syrup

Serves 6

strip of lime zest

½ cup (115 g/4 oz) caster
sugar

3 tablespoons (125 ml/4 fl oz)
Midori liqueur

½ honeydew melon, peeled
and deseeded

200 g (7 oz) green grapes,
halved

To make the syrup, place 1 cup (250 ml/8½ fl oz) water, the lime zest and sugar in a small saucepan over high heat and stir to dissolve sugar. Bring to the boil, then reduce heat to low and simmer for 5 minutes. Set aside to cool completely.

Mix together the syrup and Midori, combining well.

Using a vegetable peeler, cut long slivers of melon flesh. Combine with the grapes and place in a serving bowl or individual shallow glasses. Pour the syrup mixture over, and serve.

✿ Try a selection of green fruits, such as honeydew, grapes, kiwifruit and star fruit (carambola).

Sweet Chunky Red-bean Paste

Tsubushi-an

Makes about 2 cups

1 cup dried adzuki beans

**1½ cups (330 g/11 oz) caster
sugar**

Soak beans in a bowl of water overnight.

Drain beans. Place in a medium-sized saucepan and cover with fresh water,
bring to the boil over high heat, then drain. Return beans to the saucepan
and cover with 1.25 L (2 pt 10 fl oz) water, bring to the boil again, then
reduce heat, cover, and cook until beans are very soft, almost breaking up
(45–60 minutes). Drain well.

Return drained beans to the saucepan over low–medium heat. Stir in the
sugar and continue to stir until the beans become thick and mushy and
sugar has dissolved. Store in an airtight container in the refrigerator.

❀ This paste is a component of desserts such as rice balls with sweet red-
bean centre (page 221). It can also be served on its own, drizzled with a
little milk or cream. Or try adding a spoonful to each serving of green
tea ice (page 223).

❀ Adzuki beans are small red beans with a characteristic white marking.
They are available from Asian grocers and health food stores.

Blood-orange & Sake Granita

Serves 6

500 ml (17 fl oz) blood-orange
 juice

125 ml (4 fl oz) sake (Japanese
 rice wine)

1 blood orange, sliced,
 for garnish

GINGER SYRUP

½ cup (115 g/4 oz) caster
 sugar

a 3-cm (1¼-in) piece fresh
 ginger, thinly sliced

You will need a metal tray 2 cm (¾ in) deep and 20 cm × 30 cm (8 in × 12 in).

To make the syrup, in a small saucepan combine ½ cup (125 ml/4 fl oz) water with the sugar and ginger over high heat. Stir until sugar dissolves, bring to the boil, then reduce heat to low and simmer for 5 minutes. Set aside to cool completely. Strain syrup and discard ginger.

Combine the orange juice with the sake. Stir in ½ cup of the ginger syrup, then pour into the metal tray. Place in the freezer for 30 minutes, then run a fork through the mixture to break the ice into crystals. Repeat this process every 30 minutes until mixture becomes all ice crystals (this will take about 2–3 hours, depending how efficient your freezer is).

Spoon into chilled glasses to serve. Garnish with sliced orange.

Plums Marinated in Spiced Plum-wine Syrup

Serves 6

12 firm ripe plums (blood
   plums are ideal)

250 g (9 oz) fresh raspberries
   (optional)

candied orange peel,
   for garnish (optional)

vanilla ice-cream, to serve

PLUM-WINE SYRUP

½ cup (115 g/4 oz) caster sugar

1 cup (250 ml/8½ fl oz)
   Japanese plum wine

1 cinnamon stick

a 2-cm (¾-in) piece fresh
   ginger, sliced

strip of orange zest

To make the plum-wine syrup, place 1½ cups (375 ml/12 fl oz) water in a saucepan with the sugar, plum wine, cinnamon, ginger, and orange zest. Place over high heat, stir to dissolve the sugar, then bring to a boil. Reduce heat, simmer syrup for 10 minutes, then remove from heat and set aside to cool completely.

Slice each plum into six segments and place in a large bowl. Strain cooled syrup over the plums, toss gently to coat, and then leave for 30 minutes.

Add raspberries (if using) to the spiced plums, and spoon fruit into a serving bowl or individual dishes. Garnish with candied orange peel if desired, and serve with vanilla ice-cream.

⚜ To make candied orange peel, remove peel from half an orange and remove every scrap of pith. Cut peel into very fine strips. Place peel, ½ cup (125 ml/4 fl oz) water and 2 tablespoons (30 g/1 oz) caster sugar in a small saucepan over high heat, and stir to dissolve sugar. Reduce heat to low and simmer for 5 minutes, then remove and set aside to cool. Candied orange peel will keep for 6 months in an airtight container in a dark place. It's an ideal garnish for citrus-flavoured cakes and desserts.

⚜ Plum wine (umeshu) is a sweet liqueur flavoured with ume, a Japanese apricot (usually referred to as a plum). It is served as a refreshing drink over ice or topped with soda water, and is also used in desserts.

Rice Balls with Sweet Red-bean Centre

Ohagi

Makes 12

1 cup Japanese short-grain rice

1 cup glutinous rice

½ cup (75 g/2¾ oz) roasted soybean flour

⅓ cup (80 g/2¾ oz) caster sugar

½ cup sweet chunky red-bean paste (page 215)

Place both rices in a bowl and rinse with cold water until water runs clear. Drain well.

Combine the soybean flour and sugar in a small bowl, and set aside.

Place the mixed rices in a rice cooker (or medium-sized saucepan) with 2 cups (500 ml/17 fl oz) water, and set aside for 30 minutes.

If using rice cooker, follow manufacturer's instructions to cook rice; if using a saucepan, place over medium–high heat, cover with lid and bring to the boil, then lower heat and simmer for 12 minutes. Remove from heat and leave, with the lid on, for 10 minutes.

While rice is still very warm, use a wooden spatula to mash it until the grains start to break up and become sticky. Dampen hands in a bowl of lightly salted water, then roll rice into balls about 4 cm (1½ in) in diameter. >

Make an indentation in the ball with your thumb and fill the hollow with some red-bean paste. Reshape ball to enclose the filling, then roll the ball in the sweetened soybean flour and set aside. Repeat with remaining ingredients.

Serve with Japanese tea.

● Roasted soybean flour (kinako) is available at Asian food stores, as is prepared sweet red-bean paste.

● Glutinous rice (mochigome) is short-grained rice with grains that are white and opaque. It becomes very sticky when cooked. Japanese short-grain rice, on the other hand, has grains that are polished and translucent.

Green Tea Ice

Uji gori

Serves 6

1¾ cups (400 g/14 oz) caster
   sugar

1 tablespoon matcha
   (green-tea powder)

6 cups shaved or finely
   crushed ice

Combine the sugar and 1 cup (250 ml/8½ fl oz) water in a saucepan over high heat, stirring until sugar dissolves. Bring to the boil, then lower heat and simmer for 10 minutes or until syrup reduces to a quarter of the original volume. Set aside to cool completely.

Stir the matcha into the syrup until well combined. Place in an air-tight container and refrigerate until chilled. (It will keep for a week.)

When ready to serve, pile the ice into bowls or glasses, shaped into a peak. Stir the syrup, spoon it over the ice and serve immediately. (The syrup is also delicious over vanilla ice-cream.)

Some domestic freezer compartments have built-in settings for crushed and shaved ice. If unavailable, use an electric ice crusher (as used for making cocktails) with the setting turned to 'fine'. Or just wrap ice cubes in a clean tea towel and crush with a rolling pin or mallet.

Dumplings in a Salty–Sweet Sauce

Mitarashi dango

Serves 4–6

1 tablespoon (15 g/½ oz) potato starch or arrowroot

⅓ cup (70 g/2½ oz) caster sugar

1½ tablespoons (30 ml/1 fl oz) Japanese soy sauce

⅔ cup (115 g/4 oz) glutinous rice flour

In a small saucepan, mix the potato starch or arrowroot into ½ cup (125 ml/4 fl oz) water until smooth. Add ¼ cup (55 g/2 oz) of the sugar and the soy sauce, place over medium heat and stir. Bring to a simmer and cook for 1–2 minutes until syrupy. Set aside and keep warm.

To prepare the dumplings, combine the flour and remaining sugar in a medium-sized bowl. Using your hands, mix in only enough water – 1 tablespoon at a time, to a maximum of 6 tablespoons (120 ml/4 fl oz) – to produce a soft dough. Knead until smooth and elastic. Shape into bite-sized balls.

Bring a large saucepan of water to the boil. Cooking in batches, slide rice balls into the boiling water. The balls will sink at first: when they rise to the surface, cook for 1 minute, then remove with a slotted spoon and plunge into a bowl of cold water. Transfer to a colander lined with paper towel, and drain well.

Pour the syrup into a serving bowl and add the dumplings.

❀ Glutinous rice flour (shiratama ko) is available at Asian food stores.

Extras

Pickles (tsukemono) are an important element of Japanese dining – historically, the people's most basic meal was rice and pickles. Today, pickles are commonly used as a piquant condiment to cleanse the palate and aid digestion, but are also often served as a snack with drinks or at the tea ceremony. Just about any vegetable can be pickled, though the most popular are ginger, daikon, cucumber and eggplant.

As an accompaniment, pickles add colour, texture and flavour contrast to a meal. Other additions, such as dipping sauces, allow diners to adjust the seasoning and flavour of a dish to suit their personal taste.

Some other essential extras include steamed rice and sushi rice, the versatile thin Japanese omelette, and light-as-air tempura batter.

< Vinegared Mixed Vegetables (page 228)

Vinegared Mixed Vegetables

Makes 2 cups (serves 4 as a side dish)

200 g (7 oz) broccoli, cut into small florets

200 g (7 oz) green beans, cut into 4-cm (1½-in) lengths

½ daikon, peeled and finely grated

1 large carrot, shredded using a mandoline (use comb fitting) or cut into fine matchsticks

1 Lebanese cucumber, finely sliced

dried bonito flakes, for sprinkling (optional)

DRESSING

½ cup (125 ml/4 fl oz) Japanese rice vinegar

1 teaspoon Japanese soy sauce

2 tablespoons (30 g/1 oz) sugar

salt

Cook broccoli florets in a saucepan of boiling water for 1 minute. Remove with a slotted spoon and plunge into ice-cold water to stop the cooking process. Repeat this process with the beans. Drain vegetables well, pat dry with paper towel, and set aside.

To make the dressing, combine the vinegar, soy and sugar in a small bowl, stirring to dissolve the sugar. Add a pinch of salt, or to taste.

Gently toss all the vegetables with the dressing, to coat and combine well. Divide vegetable mix between individual bowls. If desired, sprinkle with bonito flakes for added flavour and texture.

Lightly Pickled Cabbage & Celery

Serves 4 as a starter, or as a light meal with rice

2 sticks celery, including
the leaves

¼ head white cabbage, cut
into 2-cm (¾-in) chunks

1 teaspoon salt

1 tablespoon (20 ml/¾ fl oz)
Japanese rice vinegar

2 teaspoons caster sugar

a 3-cm (1¼-in) piece fresh
ginger, peeled

1 tablespoon chopped shiso
(beefsteak plant) leaves,
or flat-leaf parsley

1 teaspoon dried bonito flakes

Japanese soy sauce,
for drizzling

Using a mandoline or very sharp knife, cut celery on the diagonal into thin slices.

Combine cabbage and celery in a ceramic or glass bowl, sprinkle with the salt, vinegar and sugar, and toss gently to combine. Place a plate on top of the vegetables and weight with some cans of food (this helps extract excess moisture). Refrigerate for 10 hours (or overnight).

Squeeze excess liquid from the vegetables using your hands. Cut the ginger into very fine slivers. Spoon the vegetables into four small dishes, sprinkle with the shiso or parsley leaves, and some bonito flakes and ginger slivers. Drizzle with soy, to taste.

Pickled Ginger

Makes 1 cup

300 g (10½ oz) young fresh ginger, unpeeled

½ teaspoon salt

1 cup (250 ml/8½ fl oz) Japanese rice vinegar

⅔ cup (145 g/5 oz) caster sugar

Wash the ginger and rub skin under cold water. (If skin does not come off easily, use a vegetable peeler.) Slice the ginger thinly on a mandoline (or use a very sharp knife), place slices in a glass or ceramic bowl, and sprinkle with the salt. Toss to combine, and leave for 1 hour.

Dry the ginger slices with paper towel, then pack into a warm, sterilised jar. Combine the rice vinegar and sugar in a small saucepan over high heat until sugar dissolves, then bring to the boil. Pour, while still hot, over the ginger slices and set aside to cool (the ginger will change colour to a light pink).

When cool, cover and seal the jar. Store in the refrigerator (the pickle will keep for 2–3 months).

- Young ginger is smooth-skinned with pink-tinged edges.
- Some commercially pickled ginger is dyed red and is considered inferior.

Sushi Rice

Makes 6 cups

2½ cups Japanese short-grain
   rice

⅓ cup (80 ml/3 fl oz) Japanese
   rice vinegar

1 tablespoon (15 g/½ oz) caster
   sugar

½ teaspoon salt

Place rice in a bowl and rinse several times until the water runs clear, then drain in a strainer for an hour.

Put the rice and 700 ml (1½ pt) water in a medium-sized saucepan. Cover with a tight-fitting lid and bring to the boil over high heat. Reduce heat to low and simmer for 15 minutes or until all the water has been absorbed. Remove pan from heat, take off lid and lay a clean tea towel across the top of the saucepan. Replace lid and set pan aside for 15 minutes.

Meanwhile, combine the vinegar, sugar and salt, stirring until sugar is dissolved. >

Empty the rice into a shallow, non-metallic tray and spread out evenly with a spatula or wooden rice paddle. Sprinkle the vinegar mixture over. Working quickly, turn the rice with the spatula or a wooden spoon, using criss-cross strokes to incorporate the vinegar mixture (don't work the rice too much, or it will become mushy). Fan the rice as you go – traditionally this is done with a flat round fan (uchiwa), but you can use any fan or even a piece of card – to remove any excess moisture and cool the rice to room temperature as quickly as possible.

Cover the prepared rice with a clean, damp tea towel. For best results, sushi rice should be used within an hour or two. If not, cover the rice and then refrigerate (but not for longer than a few hours) to prevent harmful bacteria developing.

Japanese white short-grain rice, often labelled 'sushi rice', is available in Asian food stores and supermarkets. You can cook it on the stove, as above, or in a rice cooker (following the manufacturer's instructions).

Basic Steamed Rice

Gohan

Makes about 2 cups

1 cup Japanese short-grain
  rice

Put the rice in a large bowl and rinse under cold water, swirling the rice around, until water runs clear. Drain rice and set aside in the sieve for 1 hour.

Place rice and 1 cup (250 ml/8½ fl oz) water in a medium-sized saucepan and cover with a tight-fitting lid. Place saucepan over medium heat and bring to the boil (don't lift the lid to check, as steam will escape): you will hear it boiling, and a white scum will bubble up around the edge of the lid. At this point, reduce the heat to very low and leave rice to simmer for 15 minutes or until you hear the bubbling sound subside.

Remove pan from the heat and set aside for 15 minutes with lid still on, to allow the rice to cook further in its own steam.

❀ You can use a rice cooker if you have one (follow the manufacturer's instructions).

Sesame-seed Sauce

Goma-dare

Makes 2 cups

⅓ cup white sesame seeds, freshly toasted

½ cup (125 ml/4 fl oz) Japanese soy sauce

2 tablespoons (40 ml/1½ fl oz) mirin (sweet cooking wine)

1 tablespoon (15 g/½ oz) caster sugar

1 tablespoon (20 ml/¾ fl oz) sake (Japanese rice wine)

¾ cup (180 ml/8 fl oz) dashi stock II (page 35)

Crush sesame seeds, while still warm, in a suribachi (or mortar) until finely ground. Combine soy, mirin, sugar and sake in a bowl, mix in the sesame seeds, then stir in the dashi and mix well.

This sauce is best made fresh, but can be stored in a sealed jar in the refrigerator for up to 3 days.

To toast sesame seeds, place in a dry heavy-based non-stick frying pan over medium heat. Cook for 3–5 minutes, stirring continuously, until seeds are aromatic and golden brown.

Combination Soy Sauce

Makes 1½ cups

a 10-cm (4-in) length kombu (kelp), wiped with a damp cloth

1 cup (250 ml/8½ fl oz) Japanese soy sauce

½ cup (125 ml/4 fl oz) tamari sauce

½ cup (125 ml/4 fl oz) mirin (sweet cooking wine)

2 tablespoons (30 g/1 oz) caster sugar

1 tablespoon dried bonito flakes

Place the kombu, soy and tamari in a small saucepan and set aside to soak for 1 hour.

Add the mirin and sugar to the soy mixture, place the saucepan over low heat and stir to dissolve sugar. Bring to the boil, removing the kombu just before mixture reaches boiling point. Immediately stir in the bonito flakes and remove pan from the heat at once. When the bonito flakes settle to the bottom, strain sauce through a fine mesh sieve and set aside to cool.

Store sauce in a sealed jar in the refrigerator for up to 2 weeks.

Ponzu Sauce

Makes about 2 cups

250 ml (8½ fl oz) Japanese soy
  sauce

80 ml (3 fl oz) freshly squeezed
  lime or lemon juice, or
  a combination of both

100 ml (3½ fl oz) Japanese rice
  vinegar

3 tablespoons (60 ml/2 fl oz)
  mirin (sweet cooking wine)

a 5-cm (2-in) piece kombu
  (kelp), wiped with a
  damp cloth

¼ cup dried bonito flakes

Combine all the ingredients in a glass or ceramic bowl. Cover with plastic wrap and refrigerate for 24 hours.

Pour steeped liquid through a fine sieve into a sterilised jar. Ponzu sauce will keep in a sealed jar in the refrigerator for at least 12 months.

Salad Dressing

Makes about 1 cup

1 tablespoon (20 ml/¾ fl oz)
   mirin (sweet cooking wine)
⅓ cup (80 ml/3 fl oz) Japanese
   rice vinegar
1½ tablespoons (30 ml/1 fl oz)
   Japanese soy sauce

⅔ cup (160 ml/5½ fl oz) dashi
   stock II (page 35)
1 cup dried bonito flakes

Combine the mirin, vinegar and soy in a small saucepan over medium heat, to warm through. Add the dashi, then adjust the flavour to taste, adding a little extra mirin, soy or vinegar if needed.

Bring to the boil, add the bonito flakes and remove from heat straight away. Wait for 30 seconds until the bonito flakes sink to the bottom of the pan, then pass through a strainer, discarding the bonito flakes. Leave to cool to room temperature.

This dressing will keep in a sealed jar in the refrigerator for a month.

Tempura Batter

Makes about 2 cups

1 cup (150 g/5 oz) plain flour
1 egg yolk
1 cup (250 ml/8½ fl oz) iced
  water

Prepare the batter just before use – it is best to run out and make a second batch if needed, rather than let a larger quantity sit around.

Sift the flour a few times, so that it is as light (aerated) as possible.

Place the egg yolk in a medium-sized bowl. Lightly mix with chopsticks, then stir in the iced water until combined. (The amount of water you use determines the lightness of the batter: for a lacy-looking batter, add more water. Experiment until you have a result that suits your preference.) Add the flour and stir just a few times – the mixture should be lumpy and look under-mixed (a smooth batter will *not* produce good tempura).

Salted Soy Beans

Serves 6 as a snack

**450 g (1 lb) fresh or frozen soy
  beans in the pod (edamame)**

salt

If using fresh soy beans, rub the pods with salt to remove the fine surface hairs. (This isn't necessary if you are using frozen beans.)

Bring a large saucepan of water to the boil over high heat. Add the beans, bring water back to the boil and cook for about 3 minutes or until beans are just tender. Drain.

Sprinkle beans with salt and serve warm or at room temperature. To eat, suck the beans out of the pod and discard the pod.

Salted soy beans are a traditional snack to accompany beer. In Australia, fresh soy beans can be difficult to find, but they are available frozen in most Asian food stores.

Japanese Omelette

Usuyaki tamago

Makes 3

2 eggs
½ teaspoon caster sugar
pinch of salt
vegetable oil for greasing pan

Place eggs, sugar and salt in a bowl and beat lightly using chopsticks. Pass mixture through a strainer to remove strands of egg.

Very lightly oil a Japanese omelette pan or 20-cm (8-in) non-stick frying pan and place over medium heat. Pour one-third of the egg mixture into the pan, then tilt pan quickly to spread mixture evenly over the base. Cook for 1 minute or until edges of egg mixture are dry and surface is nearly set. Using a spatula or egg flip turn the omelette over and cook for a further 5 seconds. Transfer omelette to a board.

Repeat with the remaining egg mixture to make two more thin omelettes, greasing the pan lightly between batches.

❀ These thin omelettes are used whole for wrapping ingredients, or shredded and used to garnish sushi, noodles, etc. To shred, fold the omelette into thirds and then slice very thinly into strips.

Omelette Roll

Dashimaki tamago

Makes 1 roll (serves 4 as a small dish)

3 eggs

2 tablespoons (40 ml/1½ fl oz) dashi stock II (page 35)

pinch of salt

1 teaspoon Japanese soy sauce

vegetable oil for greasing pan

1 sheet toasted nori, cut into three strips

Place eggs, dashi, salt and soy in a bowl and beat together lightly.

Lightly brush oil over the base of Japanese omelette pan or non-stick 20-cm (8-in) frying pan and place over a moderate heat. Pour one-third of the egg mixture into the pan, then tilt and swirl so eggs spread evenly to coat the base of the pan. After 10 seconds, the egg mixture should begin to set: at this point, lay a piece of nori on top. Then use chopsticks (or a spatula) to gently fold one edge of the omelette over about 5 cm (2 in). Fold over twice more to form a flat roll about 5 cm (2 in) wide.

Slide the completed roll to the far end of the pan. Lightly brush the pan with oil and add another third of the mixture, lifting the first roll slightly to allow some egg to run underneath. Again, after 10 seconds the egg should be set: lay another sheet of nori over the top and repeat the rolling process, incorporating the first roll by wrapping it into the new one. Slide the roll to the back of the pan. Repeat the oiling, cooking and rolling process with the last of the egg mixture and nori.

Carefully invert the completed roll onto a clean tea towel or bamboo mat, then gently wrap the egg roll and leave to set for 10 minutes.

Unwrap, and slice the roll crossways into four, revealing the spiral effect of the egg and nori layers. Serve as part of a main meal or bento box.

❋ To achieve a rectangular omelette if cooking in a round pan, roll the finished omelette in a bamboo sushi mat and trim away the overhanging edges.

Special Ingredients

BAINIKI A paste made from umeboshi (pickled plums).

BAMBOO SHOOTS (TAKENOKO) These mild-flavoured shoots are available canned, or sometimes fresh in Asian grocers.

BONITO FLAKES (KATSUOBUSHI) Smoked, dried and cured bonito fish, sold as shaved pieces. Used to make dashi and for garnishing.

BURDOCK ROOT (GOBO) The long, narrow root of the burdock plant. It is available fresh when in season, and frozen from Asian grocers.

DAIKON This mild-flavoured large, long white radish is used raw in salads and as a side dish. Store wrapped in plastic in the fridge to prevent it drying out. Pickled daikon is called takuan.

DASHI This essential stock forms the basis of most Japanese cooking. Instant dashi is an acceptable substitute if fresh dashi cannot be made.

EDAMAME Soy beans in the pod. Available frozen at Asian grocers, and occasionally fresh from markets.

ENOKI MUSHROOMS These mild-flavoured mushrooms come in clumps of long white slender stems with tiny round caps.

HARUSAME NOODLES Usually made from mung bean starch or potato starch, these noodles are often used in hotpots and soups.

JAPANESE MAYONNAISE Made with soy-bean oil, it is creamy with a sweet–salty taste. Available in a soft squeeze bottle in Japanese grocers.

JAPANESE MUSTARD (KARASHI) This mustard is very hot and spicy – use sparingly. It can be substituted with English mustard.

JAPANESE RICE VINEGAR (KOMESU) Japanese rice vinegar is sweeter and less acidic than other vinegars.

JAPANESE SHORT-GRAIN RICE Often sold as 'sushi rice', the grains of this short-grained rice are polished and translucent, and stick together when cooked due to the high starch content.

JAPANESE SOY SAUCE Made from soy beans, wheat and salt, Japanese soy is generally lighter and sweeter than Chinese varieties. Dark Japanese soy is often available at supermarkets. The lighter coloured version is a little saltier and is found at Asian grocers.

KAMABOKO Japanese fish cake is made from puréed fish and starch. It is served sliced and added to one-pot dishes near the end of cooking.

KANPYO (KAMPYO) Dried strips of gourd, which must be rehydrated before use. Used in hotpots, soups, and as decorative ties to secure fillings.

KOMBU (KONBU) A dried kelp seaweed that is essential for making dashi. It is covered with a white powder that contributes to the flavour and should never be washed before use, only wiped gently with a damp cloth.

KONNYAKU Made from a root vegetable called the konjac (or devil's tongue root), it is sold as a solid block of speckled jelly and has little flavour.

LOTUS ROOT A rhizome known as *renkon*. The flesh is firm and crisp and has holes through the centre. It is available frozen, vacuumed packed or canned at Asian grocers. Fresh lotus root is sometimes available, and must be cooked before eating.

MATCHA (MACCHA) A green powder made from the highest-quality green tea. It is the essential ingredient for the Japanese tea ceremony and is also used as a flavouring for soba noodles and desserts.

MIRIN A sweet rice wine used in cooking to tenderise and sweeten. It is widely available at supermarkets and Asian food stores.

MISO PASTE Made from fermented soy beans, miso has myriad uses. The paste will keep, refrigerated in a sealed container, for up to a year. Miso comes in a variety of colours: in general, the darker the colour the more salty the taste. The most commonly used are **white miso** (shiromiso), and **red miso** (akamiso). **Brown-rice miso** (sendai miso) is a dark, robust miso made from brown rice and soy beans.

MITSUBA Also known as trefoil or Japanese parsley, this herb has a light peppery flavour. If unavailable, substitute with flat-leaf parsley.

MIZUNA A large-leafed herb with a peppery flavour. Use rocket as a substitute.

NORI Dried paper-like sheets of pounded seaweed. It is sold in sheets, strips or flakes (ao-nori). Buy it pre-toasted, or toast it yourself by quickly passing a sheet over a gas flame three times.

PANKO Dried white breadcrumbs used as a coating for deep-fried food. Available at Japanese grocers.

PICKLED GINGER (GARI) Pickled ginger is used as a palate cleanser and garnish. It usually accompanies sashimi and sushi.

PONZU SAUCE A dipping sauce made from soy, bonito, other flavourings, and lemon or lime juice. You can buy it or make your own (page 237).

POTATO STARCH Used as a thickening agent for sauces and for coating foods before frying. It is a cheaper option than katakuriko (starch made from the stem of the katakuri lily), which was traditionally used.

SAKE Japanese rice wine with a similar taste to a very dry sherry. Cooking-grade sake is used as a tenderiser and suppresses saltiness. Drinking sake is more refined, and may be served warm, chilled or at room temperature.

SANCHO PEPPER The ground seeds of the Japanese prickly ash. It has a spicy, tangy flavour and is used for seasoning.

SESAME OIL An oil extracted from toasted sesame seeds. It has an intense flavour and is used in small amounts in dressings and when frying.

SESAME SEEDS (GOMA) Both white and black sesame seeds are used in Japanese cuisine. Toasting enhances the flavour.

SHICHIMI TOGARASHI A mixture of seven spices. Generally includes sancho pepper, sesame seeds, shiso, Japanese mustard and hot red chilli.

SHIITAKE MUSHROOMS These mushrooms have a smooth dark-brown cap with curled edges. They have a strong flavour. Available fresh and dried.

SHIRATAKI NOODLES Commonly used in hotpots, these noodles have little taste or nutritional value but absorb the flavours of other ingredients.

SHISO Also known as oba or perilla, this large-leafed herb is from the mint family. The flavour is refreshing and quite similar to basil.

SOBA NOODLES These noodles are made from buckwheat flour. Available dried, and sometimes fresh, in Japanese grocers and some supermarkets.

SOY BEANS These beans are a rich source of protein and are an important part of Japanese cuisine. They are available (fresh or frozen) in the pod, canned or dried. Dried beans need to be soaked before cooking.

TAMARI A wheat-free soy sauce. It is thicker and darker than Japanese soy.

TOFU Also known as bean curd, tofu is the set 'milk' made from grinding soy beans and then soaking them in water. **Silken tofu** has a soft custard-like consistency and is used in sauces, or eaten as is with simple toppings such as soy sauce and ginger. **Firm tofu** is made from pressed curds and is much denser, making it suitable for grilling, stir-frying and simmering. **Silken firm tofu** is midway in texture, and can be deep-fried or used in salads and soups.

UDON NOODLES These white wheat noodles are usually used in soups. They're available in different thicknesses, and can be bought fresh or dried.

UMEBOSHI A pickled apricot (often referred to as a Japanese plum), often served as an accompaniment to rice or used in dressings.

WAKAME A delicate-tasting, curly-leafed seaweed. It is sold in dried form and must be rehydrated before use. Commonly used in miso and salads.

WASABI PASTE A condiment made from the ground root of the wasabi plant. You can buy it as a paste, or as a powder that is mixed with water to make a paste. It has a hot spicy flavour similar to horseradish.

Conversions

Important note: All cup and spoon measures given in this book are based on Australian standards. The most important thing to remember is that an Australian cup = 250 ml, while an American cup = 237 ml and a British cup = 284 ml. Also, an Australian tablespoon is equivalent to 4 teaspoons, not 3 teaspoons as in the United States and Britain. US equivalents have been provided throughout for all liquid cup/spoon measures. Equivalents for dry ingredients measured in cups/spoons have been included for flour, sugar and rising agents such as baking powder. For other dry ingredients (chopped vegetables, nuts, etc.), American cooks should be generous with their cup measures – slight variations in quantities of such ingredients are unlikely to affect results.

VOLUME

Australian cups/spoons	Millilitres	US fluid ounces
* 1 teaspoon	5 ml	
1 tablespoon (4 teaspoons)	20 ml	¾ fl oz
1½ tablespoons	30 ml	1 fl oz
2 tablespoons	40 ml	1½ fl oz
¼ cup	60 ml	2 fl oz
⅓ cup	80 ml	3 fl oz
½ cup	125 ml	4 fl oz
¾ cup	180 ml	6 fl oz
1 cup	250 ml	8½ fl oz
4 cups	1 L	34 fl oz

*the volume of a teaspoon is the same around the world

SIZE

Centimetres	Inches
1 cm	⅜ in
2 cm	¾ in
2.5 cm	1 in
5 cm	2 in
10 cm	4 in
15 cm	6 in
20 cm	8 in
30 cm	12 in

TEMPERATURE

Celsius	Fahrenheit
150°C	300°F
160°C	320°F
170°C	340°F
180°C	360°F
190°C	375°F
200°C	390°F
210°C	410°F
220°C	420°F

WEIGHT

Grams	Ounces
15 g	½ oz
30 g	1 oz
60 g	2 oz
85 g	3 oz
110 g	4 oz
140 g	5 oz
170 g	6 oz
200 g	7 oz
225 g	8 oz (½ lb)
450 g	16 oz (1 lb)
500 g	1 lb 2 oz
900 g	2 lb
1 kg	2 lb 3 oz

Index

LONDON, NEW YORK, MUNICH,
MELBOURNE and DELHI

First published in Great Britain in 2011 by
Dorling Kindersley, 80 Strand, London, WC2R 0RL

A Penguin Company

Published by Penguin Group (Australia), 2010
250 Camberwell Road, Camberwell, Victoria 3124, Australia
(a division of Pearson Australia Group Pty Ltd)

10 9 8 7 6 5 4 3 2 1

Text and photographs copyright © Penguin Group (Australia), 2010

Cover design by Nikki Townsend © Penguin Group (Australia)
Text design by Claire Tice and Marley Flory © Penguin Group (Australia)
Photography by Julie Renouf
Food styling by Lee Blaylock
Typeset in Nimbus Sans Novus by Post Pre-press Group, Brisbane, Queensland
Scanning and separations by Splitting Image P/L, Clayton, Victoria
Printed and bound in China by Everbest Printing Co. Ltd

A CIP catalogue record for this book is available from the British Library.

ISBN: 978-1-4053-6326-6

Discover more at www.dk.com